MW01064026

How Should Husbands Treat
Their Wives?

HUSBANDS
LOVE YOUR WIVES

The Bible's View of the
Family Series

EDWARD D. ANDREWS

HUSBANDS LOVE YOUR WIVES

Edward D. Andrews

Christian Publishing House

Cambridge, Ohio

CHRISTIAN
PUBLISHING
HOUSE

FOUNDED 2005

Unless otherwise stated, Scripture quotations are from Updated American Standard Version (UASV) Copyright © 2022 by Christian Publishing House

HUSBANDS LOVE YOUR WIVES: How Should Husbands Treat Their Wives? by Edward D. Andrews

ISBN-10: 194575754X

ISBN-13: 978-1945757549

Table of Contents

Edward D. Andrews

Book Description

In an era where marriages face challenges from all sides, "HUSBANDS LOVE Your WIVES: How Should Husbands Treat Their Wives?" offers a Scriptural roadmap for men striving to emulate the love and leadership demonstrated by Christ. As the Apostle Paul has outlined, the husband is the head of the wife just as Christ is the head of the church. This headship is not one of tyranny or arbitrary rule but one characterized by love, respect, and spiritual guidance.

In this comprehensive guide, each chapter focuses on a distinct principle or practice crucial for husbands to internalize. The book begins by laying the foundation with "The Head of a Woman Is the Man," where the Biblical view of a husband's role is carefully examined. Following chapters delve into gaining deep respect from one's spouse, the two keys to a lasting marriage, and how to build a strong and happy marital relationship.

Through chapters like "Husbands—Recognize Christ's Headship," the book underscores the essentiality of acknowledging the ultimate Headship of Christ over every Christian institution, including the family. Understanding the weight of this responsibility, the book provides "Wise Guidance for Married Couples" and elaborates on "Godly Conduct Within the Family Circle," helping men to lead their families in accordance with Biblical precepts.

Children are not left out of the equation. With a chapter dedicated to training your child from infancy, the book provides essential tools to help instill a love for God and His Word from a young age. In a world filled with destructive influences, the book equips husbands to "Protect Your Family From Destructive Influences," emphasizing the role of the husband as the spiritual watchman of his household.

With a view that a loving husband cultivates a wife who is "Dearly Loved," the book offers not just theoretical knowledge but practical steps in showing self-sacrificing love, maintaining peace in the household, and doing one's part to promote a happy family life.

Drawing from an objective Historical-Grammatical method of Scriptural interpretation, "HUSBANDS LOVE Your WIVES" is a must-read for every Christian husband committed to fulfilling his God-ordained role in the marriage. It is not only a book for married men but also for those contemplating marriage, as it sets the stage for what God expects and how immense the rewards are—both in this life and in the life to come—when His design for marital roles is followed.

Whether you are a newlywed seeking guidance or a husband of many years wishing to enhance your marital relationship, this book serves as a timeless resource grounded firmly in the Word of God.

Preface

Dear Reader,

Thank you for picking up this book, "HUSBANDS LOVE Your WIVES: How Should Husbands Treat Their Wives?" The decision to read this work signifies not only a personal commitment to understanding the divine blueprint for marital relationships but also a willingness to actively engage in shaping a home built on the cornerstones of Christian faith.

This book was born out of a need to address a critical aspect of Christian living that is often misunderstood or taken for granted: the role of a husband in a marital relationship. While society offers a myriad of perspectives on what it means to be a good husband, this book aims to delve into what the Scriptures specifically say about this vital role.

We live in times where marriages are strained by economic pressures, social influences, and even ideological differences. Moreover, the erosion of faith in many sectors has led to confusion regarding the roles and responsibilities within the Christian household. Given these circumstances, this book endeavors to be more than just a compilation of advice; it seeks to be a manual, deeply rooted in Scripture, for husbands who aspire to lead their families in a manner that aligns with God's Word.

The chapters are organized to provide not only a foundational understanding of the Biblical concept of a husband's role but also practical guidance on implementing these principles in daily life. As you will find, topics cover a broad range—from understanding headship in a Biblical context to ensuring that your home remains a sanctuary against destructive influences.

As the writer of Ephesians beautifully puts it, "Husbands, love your wives, just as Christ also loved the church and gave Himself up for her" (Ephesians 5:25, UASV). The ultimate aim of this book is to help husbands gain insights into what this self-sacrificing love looks like in daily actions, decisions, and responsibilities.

While the journey toward being a husband after God's own heart may be filled with challenges, the rewards—emotional, spiritual, and eternal—are immeasurable. May this book serve as an invaluable companion on that journey, providing both enlightenment and encouragement grounded in the unchanging truths of Scripture.

In Christian Love,

Edward D. Andrews

Author of 220+ books and Chief Translator of the Updated American Standard Version

Edward D. Andrews

Introduction

Welcome to "HUSBANDS LOVE Your WIVES: How Should Husbands Treat Their Wives?" As you turn these pages, you are taking a step on a transformative path, one that aims to realign our often skewed human perspectives with the clear, unchanging wisdom found in the Scriptures. While the Preface laid out the necessity and the underpinnings for this book, and the Book Description offered you an overview of the topics covered, this Introduction aims to set the stage for the exploration that lies ahead.

Marriage, as instituted by Jehovah, is not merely a social contract or a personal arrangement for mutual comfort. It's far more profound, serving as a living testament to divine principles and God's purpose for humankind. However, to fulfill this purpose, each participant—husband and wife—must understand their respective roles. While the focus of this book is on the role of husbands, it is crucial to remember that a husband's role can only be properly understood in the context of his relationship with his wife and, above all, with Christ.

The objective of this book is twofold. First, it seeks to dispel the myths and misconceptions that often surround the notion of "headship" within the family structure. Rest assured, Biblical headship is not about domineering control or old-fashioned patriarchy; it is about loving leadership, sacrificial giving, and spiritual direction. Second, this book offers practical application points derived directly from Scripture. These are not merely human opinions or psychological theories but time-tested truths grounded in the Word of God.

Our exploration will cover a comprehensive range of topics—from the philosophical to the practical. Whether it is gaining deep respect from your wife or protecting your family from destructive influences, each chapter is designed to tackle an aspect of marital life that is relevant, if not critical, to your role as a husband.

As you progress through this book, you'll find that the core principles are supported by concrete scriptural references, primarily drawn from the UASV. These are not just to substantiate what is written but to urge you to further personal study.

So, with a humble and open heart, I invite you to join this exploration of one of the most pivotal roles a man can undertake in his life—that of a husband. Armed with the Word of God and a willingness to apply it, you are well on your way to becoming the husband Jehovah has called you to be, benefiting not just yourself but your family and, indeed, your relationship with God Himself.

May your journey through these pages be enlightening, challenging, and ultimately rewarding, leading to a more fulfilling marriage that glorifies God.

In the pages that follow, let us dig deeply into the Scriptures to find the hidden treasures of wisdom that Jehovah has stored for those who seek to obey Him in their marital roles. Let us begin.

CHAPTER 1 The Head of a Woman Is the Man

Considerations for a Single Sister in Choosing a Marriage Mate

As a single sister contemplating marriage, the gravity of this life-altering decision cannot be overstated. The Scriptures have much to say about the marital relationship and the qualities to look for in a prospective spouse. Given the magnitude of this commitment, it is imperative to be informed and discerning in one's choice.

Is He a Devoted Christian?

First and foremost, the question of spirituality should be at the top of your list. **Is he a devoted Christian?** The Apostle Paul was very clear on this matter when he said, "Do not be yoked together with unbelievers" (2 Corinthians 6:14, UASV). This is not a light admonition but an essential criterion. If a man is not devoted to God, how can he be expected to be devoted to his family, following the principles laid out in Scripture?

What is His View on Headship?

The concept of *headship* is vital in Christian marriage. Ephesians 5:23 states, "For the husband is the head of the wife even as Christ is the head of the church, his body, and is himself its Savior." What is his understanding of this Biblical principle? Does he view it as a platform for authoritarian rule or as a responsibility to lovingly guide, protect, and nourish his family as Christ does the church?

How Does He Treat Others?

Character is often revealed in how one treats others, especially those from whom he has nothing to gain. Jesus said, "By this everyone will know that you are my disciples, if you love one another" (John 13:35, UASV). How does he treat his family, his friends, and even strangers? Is he kind, respectful, and compassionate? These qualities are not only desirable but essential in a Christian marriage mate.

What Are His Moral and Ethical Standards?

Scriptural standards of morality should not be compromised. Paul's letter to the Corinthians warns against various kinds of immoral behavior (1 Corinthians 6:9-10). Does he display high moral and ethical standards in his dealings with others? Is he honest, trustworthy, and pure in his intentions and actions?

Is He Hardworking and Responsible?

The Apostle Paul stipulates in 2 Thessalonians 3:10 that "if anyone is not willing to work, let him not eat." In a marriage, both partners need to contribute to the family's welfare. Is he diligent in his secular responsibilities? Is he financially responsible, avoiding debt and managing resources wisely? These are crucial factors for long-term marital success.

What Are His Views on Family and Children?

Marriage often leads to family. What are his views on children and on his role as a potential father? The Biblical mandate to "Train up a child in the way he should go"

(Proverbs 22:6, UASV) cannot be fulfilled if he is not fully invested in the spiritual, emotional, and physical well-being of his future children.

How Does He Handle Conflict and Disagreements?

No marriage is without conflict, but how conflicts are resolved is telling of one's character and the health of the relationship. The Apostle Paul encourages Christians to "Let all bitterness and wrath and anger and clamor and slander be put away from you, along with all malice" (Ephesians 4:31, UASV). Does he handle disagreements with humility, seeking resolution rather than victory?

This is by no means an exhaustive list, but these questions serve as essential guideposts in evaluating a prospective marriage mate. The aim is not to scrutinize someone for faults, but to assess whether both of you are aligned in your core beliefs and values, as outlined in Scripture. In doing so, you prepare the groundwork for a union that honors God and fosters mutual love, respect, and lasting happiness.

Challenges Faced by Wives in a Christian Marriage

Christian marriage, while a divinely sanctioned institution, is not without its challenges. For wives, some of these challenges are particular to their roles and responsibilities as outlined in the Scriptures. Let's delve into some of the more common obstacles they might face, always mindful that our foundation for understanding these issues comes directly from the inspired Word of God.

Submission to Headship

14

Perhaps one of the most challenging aspects of a Christian marriage for a wife is the Biblical injunction to be submissive to her husband. The Apostle Paul writes, "*Wives, submit to your own husbands, as to the Lord*" (Ephesians 5:22, UASV). In a society that often misunderstands or outright rejects the idea of submission, embracing this divine principle can be difficult. Submission here is not synonymous with servitude but is about recognizing a God-appointed structure within the household. The challenge arises when husbands misunderstand their role, leading to imbalances and dissatisfaction.

Balancing Career and Family

Proverbs 31:10-31 lauds the industrious woman who takes care of her home and also engages in fruitful labor. In our modern context, many women find themselves torn between their careers and their Biblical role within the family. *The challenge is finding the right balance* between fulfilling occupational aspirations and adhering to familial responsibilities as outlined in the Scriptures.

Spiritual Partnership and Nurturing

A wife has a role in nurturing the spiritual climate of her household. The challenge is how to do this without undermining the husband's role as the spiritual leader, especially when she might be more spiritually mature or knowledgeable. 1 Peter 3:1-2 offers a solution, suggesting that wives can win over their husbands "without a word" through their conduct. *The challenge lies in the application of this principle*, particularly when it comes to complex spiritual matters.

Handling Conflict Righteously

Conflict is inevitable in any relationship, including marriage. The way a wife handles disagreements can either build up or tear down her household. Paul's advice to "*Let all bitterness and wrath and anger and clamor and slander be put away from you, along with all malice*" (Ephesians 4:31, UASV) is universal but may be particularly poignant for wives, who often find themselves in the role of peacekeepers.

Sexual Intimacy and Moral Boundaries

1 Corinthians 7:3-5 talks about the mutual responsibilities of husbands and wives concerning sexual intimacy. This area often poses challenges for women, especially when cultural and social norms about sexuality conflict with Biblical principles. *The challenge is maintaining sexual integrity and fulfilling marital responsibilities* while still upholding one's personal dignity and spiritual values.

Dealing with External Pressures and Expectations

From societal pressures to cultural expectations, external factors can put a strain on the Christian wife's ability to fulfill her Biblical roles. The Scriptures encourage us to be "not conformed to this world" (Romans 12:2, UASV), but living that out practically as a wife and possibly a mother can be complex and mentally taxing.

While these challenges are significant, they are not insurmountable. Through prayer, Bible study, and applying Biblical principles, a wife can not only overcome these obstacles but also thrive in her role. Marriage, after all, is a partnership where both husband and wife are "heirs together of the grace of life" (1 Peter 3:7, UASV). By leaning on Jehovah and the principles found in His Word, a wife can navigate these challenges in a way that honors both God and her spouse.

The Biblical Rationale for a Wife Choosing to Be Subject to Her Husband

Choosing to be subject to one's husband is not merely a cultural norm or a tradition to be blindly followed; it is a Biblically-grounded principle with deep theological and practical implications. In this discussion, we'll explore the myriad reasons, rooted in Scripture, why a Christian wife would make such a choice.

God's Divine Ordination

First and foremost, the reason a Christian wife chooses to be subject to her husband is that *this arrangement is divinely ordained by God.* The Apostle Paul emphasizes this in Ephesians 5:22-24, stating: "Wives, submit to your own husbands, as to the Lord. For the husband is the head of the wife even as Christ is the head of the church, his body, and is himself its Savior. Now as the church submits to Christ, so also wives should submit in everything to their husbands" (UASV). When a wife submits to her husband, she is actually submitting to Jehovah's arrangement, and by extension, to Jehovah Himself.

Reflecting Christ and the Church

The marital relationship is designed to be a reflection of the relationship between Christ and the Church. In submitting to her husband, a wife is mirroring the Church's submission to Christ. This is not a demeaning or inferior role but one of great responsibility and honor. As Ephesians 5:32 reveals, this mystery is profound, and it reflects Christ and the Church. By choosing to be subject to her husband, the wife participates in this divine representation, giving testimony to the heavenly truths it signifies.

17

Fostering Unity and Peace

Submission also contributes to family unity and peace. When every member of the family fulfills their God-given role, the home functions more smoothly. Paul writes in 1 Corinthians 14:33 that "God is not a God of confusion but of peace" (UASV). *When a wife subjects herself to her husband, she is contributing to the peace and order that God wishes to be characteristic of Christian households.*

A Means of Witness

A wife's respectful and submissive behavior can serve as a powerful Christian witness, especially when the husband is not a believer. Peter advises: "In the same way, wives, be in subjection to your own husbands, so that even if any are not obedient to the word, they may be won without a word by the conduct of their wives" (1 Peter 3:1, UASV). Thus, a wife's submission could be an effective means of evangelism within her own home.

Love and Respect

Ephesians 5:33 concludes by stating that "each one of you must also love his wife as he loves himself, and the wife must respect her husband" (UASV). Mutual respect and love are fundamental to the marital relationship. A wife's choice to be subject to her husband can be seen as an expression of this respect, just as the husband's love for his wife is an expression of his devotion to her well-being.

Safety and Well-Being

In a godly marriage, a husband is to love his wife "just as Christ also loved the church and gave himself up for her" (Ephesians 5:25, UASV). A husband thus has a solemn responsibility to protect and care for his wife. Her submission is not a concession to vulnerability but a recognition of a protective arrangement.

A Christian wife chooses to be subject to her husband not because she is inferior or less capable, but because she is obedient to God's Word and design for marriage. This submission is aimed at reflecting Christ's relationship with the Church, maintaining peace and unity in the home, and upholding a powerful Christian witness. Above all, it is an act of obedience and worship to Jehovah, who created the marital arrangement for our benefit and His glory.

The Role of Headship in a Christian Marriage: A Biblical Perspective

The issue of headship in marriage is often misunderstood or misconstrued, especially in contemporary society. Yet, the Bible is clear about who holds the headship in the marital relationship and the underlying reasons behind this divinely-ordained structure. This exposition aims to clarify these points exhaustively.

The Scriptural Foundation for Headship in Marriage

The Scripture unequivocally states that the husband is the head of the wife. Paul writes in Ephesians 5:23, "*For the husband is the head of the wife even as Christ is the head of the church, his body, and is himself its Savior*" (UASV). This headship is not a product of human tradition but is grounded in God's created order and divine design.

Is the Headship Oppressive?

The idea that a husband's headship implies an oppressive or domineering relationship with his wife is a misconception often perpetuated by misunderstanding the Biblical text. *The concept of headship in the Bible is about loving leadership, not autocratic control.* The husband's role is modeled after Christ's relationship with the Church. Ephesians 5:25 makes it clear that husbands should love their wives "*as Christ loved the church and gave himself up for her.*"

Does It Make the Wife Inferior?

Headship does not imply inferiority. Both the husband and wife are made in the image of God (Genesis 1:27) and are "heirs together of the grace of life" (1 Peter 3:7, UASV). The Apostle Paul further emphasizes this equality in Galatians 3:28, "*There is neither Jew nor Greek, there is neither slave nor free, there is no male and female, for you are all one in Christ Jesus.*" *Headship and submission are about function and role, not worth or value.*

Deep Respect for the Wife

While the Scripture calls for wives to be in subjection to their husbands, it also clearly states that husbands should hold their wives in deep respect. Ephesians 5:28-29 states, "*In the same way husbands should love their wives as their own bodies. He who loves his wife loves himself. For no one ever hated his own flesh, but nourishes and cherishes it, just as Christ does the church.*"

When a husband understands his role of loving leadership modeled after Christ, it fosters a relationship in which the wife feels deeply respected and valued. *This is not a one-sided subjugation but a mutual uplifting within the parameters set by God.* In such an environment, the wife's submission is a voluntary act of love and respect in response to her husband's loving leadership, not a demeaning obligation.

The Bible's teaching on marital headship is neither oppressive nor demeaning to the wife. On the contrary, it sets the stage for a fulfilling, loving relationship grounded in mutual respect and divine wisdom. By adhering to these divinely ordained roles and principles, both the husband and wife can experience a marriage that honors Jehovah and brings deep and lasting joy to both parties.

Lessons on Subjection in Marriage from Jesus, Abigail, and Mary

Understanding the principles of subjection in marriage is crucial for Christian husbands and wives. In this discussion, we will delve into the lives of Jesus, Abigail, and Mary, the wife of Joseph and the mother of Jesus, to glean profound insights on this topic.

Learning from Jesus: The Ultimate Model of Subjection

Christ's Relationship with the Father

Jesus Christ, although equal with the Father in nature and essence (John 10:30), chose to submit Himself to the Father's will. This is evident in Scriptures such as John 5:30, where Jesus says, "*I seek not my own will but the will of him who sent me.*"

Lessons for Husbands

For husbands, Jesus' model teaches the art of loving leadership. Christ's subjection to the Father was never a diminishment of His worth, but an exemplification of perfect love, humility, and obedience. Similarly, husbands should exercise their headship not as tyrants but as loving leaders, always seeking the well-being of their wives (Ephesians 5:25).

Lessons for Wives

For wives, Christ's submission illuminates the beauty of voluntary submission. Just as Christ submitted to the Father out of love and obedience, wives are called to submit to their husbands in a manner that honors God (Ephesians 5:22).

Learning from Abigail: Wisdom and Tactfulness in Subjection

Abigail's Quick Thinking

The story of Abigail is found in 1 Samuel 25. Abigail, the wife of Nabal, displayed incredible wisdom and tactfulness when she intercepted David and his men, preventing an unnecessary bloodbath.

Lessons for Husbands

For husbands, Abigail's story highlights the importance of valuing their wives' input and wisdom. A husband's headship doesn't negate the need for counsel and wisdom, which may very well come from his wife.

Lessons for Wives

For wives, Abigail's action illustrates how submission and wisdom can co-exist. She took initiative in a critical situation while maintaining a submissive and respectful attitude toward her husband and toward David.

Learning from Mary: Unquestioning Obedience in Difficult Circumstances

Mary's Unwavering Faith

The story of Mary, the mother of Jesus, offers a remarkable example of subjection. Faced with an extraordinary mandate from God to become the mother of the Messiah, Mary responded, "*Behold, I am the servant of the Lord; let it be to me according to your word*" (Luke 1:38, UASV).

Lessons for Husbands

For husbands, Mary's story teaches the importance of compassionate understanding. Joseph initially considered divorcing her quietly but chose to stand by her when he understood the divine plan (Matthew 1:18-25). *Compassionate understanding enhances the effectiveness of headship.*

Lessons for Wives

For wives, Mary's example underscores the significance of trust and obedience, even when the path ahead seems uncertain or fraught with difficulties. Her subjection to God's will and to her husband Joseph was a testament to her deep faith.

The lives of Jesus, Abigail, and Mary offer invaluable lessons on the principles of subjection in marriage. From Jesus, we learn the essence of loving leadership and willing submission. Abigail teaches us the importance of wisdom and tactfulness within the bounds of subjection, while Mary exemplifies unquestioning obedience and trust. By studying and applying these Biblical examples, Christian husbands and wives can better understand and embody the divine principle of subjection, thereby honoring Jehovah and enriching their marital relationship.

Facilitating the Wife's Role in a Christian Family: Biblical Insights

Understanding the Biblical framework for the role of the wife in a Christian family is vital for a harmonious and godly household. When a wife finds it easier to fulfill her role, it invariably leads to a more blessed family unit. Here, we will discuss various factors and Biblical principles that can assist a wife in this endeavor.

Spiritual Formation and Personal Relationship with God

Source of Strength

The Apostle Paul encouraged all Christians, including wives, to "*be strengthened by the grace that is in Christ Jesus*" (2 Timothy 2:1, UASV). A wife's primary source of strength should be her relationship with Jehovah and His Son, Jesus Christ.

Lessons for the Wife

Prioritizing spiritual formation makes it easier for a wife to be in alignment with Scriptural principles. Daily Bible study, prayer, and meditation help cultivate qualities like love, patience, and kindness, which are indispensable in fulfilling her role (Galatians 5:22-23).

The Importance of Mutual Respect and Love

The Husband's Role

The Scripture instructs husbands to love their wives *"as their own bodies"* (Ephesians 5:28, UASV). When a husband follows this Biblical directive, he creates an atmosphere that makes it easier for his wife to be submissive.

Lessons for the Wife

A loving and respectful environment fosters willing submission. When a wife feels loved and respected, she naturally finds it easier to be in subjection to her husband, as instructed in Ephesians 5:22.

Open Communication and Emotional Support

The Principle of Honest Dialogue

Colossians 3:9 instructs Christians to *"Stop lying to one another"* and to practice honest communication. This extends to the marital relationship as well.

Lessons for the Wife

Open, honest communication helps address issues, alleviates misunderstandings, and promotes emotional well-being. Emotional support from her husband further makes it easier for a wife to fulfill her responsibilities effectively.

Partnership in Parenting and Household Duties

Shared Responsibility

Proverbs 31 presents the virtuous woman as one who takes an active role in the welfare of her household.

However, her tasks are not a burden but are part of a partnership with her husband.

Lessons for the Wife

The sharing of responsibilities creates a more manageable environment for the wife. When a husband involves himself in parenting and household duties, he not only adheres to Biblical principles but also eases the burden on his wife.

A Community of Faith: The Role of the Church

Spiritual Fellowship

Hebrews 10:24-25 encourages Christians to associate with one another for mutual encouragement. This principle is equally applicable within the context of marriage and family.

Lessons for the Wife

Being part of a godly community can offer additional layers of support and accountability. This can make it easier for a wife to fulfill her role, as she can glean wisdom and encouragement from other godly women in the congregation.

To make it easier for a wife to fulfill her role in a Christian family, various factors come into play: her personal spirituality, mutual respect and love in the marriage, open communication, shared responsibilities, and a supportive church community. When these elements are in place, they align with Biblical principles, facilitating the wife's role and contributing to a harmonious Christian household that glorifies Jehovah.

The Comprehensive Role of the Christian Husband: A Biblical Examination

Understanding the multi-faceted role of a Christian husband is indispensable for building a family that aligns with God's Word. The Scripture outlines that a husband is expected to provide for the spiritual, emotional, and material needs of his family. Let's delve deeper into each of these aspects in light of Biblical instruction.

Spiritual Leadership: The Foremost Responsibility

God's Directive for Spiritual Leadership

Paul wrote to the Ephesian church saying, "*Husbands, love your wives, just as Christ also loved the congregation and gave himself up for her*" (Ephesians 5:25, UASV). The Scripture places a high premium on the spiritual well-being of the family, and the husband has the primary responsibility in this domain.

Lessons for the Husband

As a spiritual leader, the husband should guide the family in worship, Bible study, and prayer. Just like Joshua resolved, "*As for me and my house, we will serve Jehovah*" (Joshua 24:15), a husband must take the initiative in spiritual matters. He must be a model of godliness, leading by example and providing spiritual direction for his family.

Emotional Well-being: A Sanctuary of Support and Love

The Mandate for Emotional Nourishment

Colossians 3:19 specifically instructs husbands, "*do not be embittered against them [your wives]*," emphasizing the need to be emotionally supportive.

Lessons for the Husband

Emotional well-being is not an optional luxury but a Scriptural mandate. A husband must be a pillar of emotional support, providing love, encouragement, and kindness. Being "*quick to listen, slow to speak, slow to anger*" (James 1:19) enables a husband to understand and address the emotional needs of his family better.

Material Provision: Not Just a Social Construct but a Divine Command

The Biblical Injunction for Material Provision

"*But if anyone does not provide for his own, and especially for those of his household, he has denied the faith and is worse than an unbeliever*" (1 Timothy 5:8, UASV). This is a stern warning and a clear mandate for Christian husbands.

Lessons for the Husband

Material provision is a Scriptural obligation, not merely a societal expectation. This entails providing not just the basic necessities like food and shelter but also a stable and secure environment for the family to flourish.

The Balanced Approach: Harmonizing Spiritual, Emotional, and Material Care

The Integrated Model

1 Peter 3:7 exhorts husbands to live *"with your wives in an understanding way,"* which encapsulates the idea of a balanced, comprehensive care.

Lessons for the Husband

Each aspect—spiritual, emotional, and material—cannot be isolated but must be integrated for holistic family well-being. While material provision is crucial, it shouldn't overshadow spiritual guidance and emotional support, and vice versa.

God has laid down comprehensive guidelines for what He expects from Christian husbands. These responsibilities are not merely guidelines but commandments for ensuring the holistic well-being of a Christian family. By diligently adhering to these divine principles, a Christian husband fulfills his God-given role and brings glory to God. This balanced approach serves as the bedrock for a harmonious, godly household.

What Christian Husbands Can Learn About Valuing Their Wives: A Biblical Analysis

Understanding God's view of women and the virtuous qualities enumerated in Proverbs 31 can offer husbands a profound perspective on how to value and treat their wives. These Scriptures are not just proverbs or idealized views; they are God-breathed principles for a fulfilling and godly marital life.

Edward D. Andrews

(a) The Way God Views Women: Dignified and Equally Valuable

God's Creation of Woman: An Equal and Complementary Partner

The account of creation in Genesis sets the stage for understanding God's view of women. The woman was created as a "helper" suitable for the man (Genesis 2:18, UASV). *This doesn't imply inferiority but denotes complementarity.* The term "helper" ('ezer') used in Hebrew suggests a supportive, but by no means a secondary role.

The Dignity Bestowed by Jesus

Jesus Christ treated women with immense respect and dignity, breaking away from cultural norms that marginalized them. His interaction with women—from dialogues with the Samaritan woman to His attitude towards Mary Magdalene—shows a complete absence of discrimination (John 4:4-26, Luke 8:2).

Lessons for Husbands

Husbands can learn to view their wives as God does: equally valuable, imbued with dignity, and deserving of respect. This perspective should shape the husband's behavior, ensuring he gives his wife the respect and dignity she inherently deserves as a creation of God.

(b) Wisdom from Proverbs 31: The Virtuous Wife

The Virtuous Woman: A Panorama of Qualities

Proverbs 31:10-31 portrays the ideal virtues a woman can possess. From being a hard worker to having the fear of

Jehovah, the passage covers various facets of a virtuous woman's life.

Unfading Beauty and Value

The passage concludes with a compelling statement: *"Charm may be deceptive, and beauty does not last, but a woman who fears Jehovah is to be praised"* (Proverbs 31:30, UASV). *This suggests that the ultimate virtue lies in fearing Jehovah, transcending all external qualities.*

Lessons for Husbands

Proverbs 31 should serve as a mirror for husbands, reflecting how they should appreciate their wives. Recognizing these virtues in their wives, and valuing them for these qualities, is a step towards fulfilling the husband's Biblical role. This recognition should manifest in praise, emotional support, and most importantly, spiritual leadership to help her grow in her relationship with Jehovah.

Balancing Both Perspectives: The Comprehensive View

Blending the high regard that God has for women and the virtues listed in Proverbs 31 creates a harmonious understanding of how a husband should treat his wife. Both perspectives are intertwined and serve to enrich the spiritual, emotional, and relational aspects of a Christian marriage.

The teachings from Scriptures regarding God's view on women and the Proverbs 31 description provide husbands with a treasure trove of wisdom. By aligning with these Biblical teachings, husbands not only enrich their marital relationships but also please Jehovah, the Originator of the divine institution of marriage.

Edward D. Andrews

CHAPTER 2 A Husband Who Gains Deep Respect

The Imperative of Ephesians 5:33 for Husbands: A Detailed Examination

Ephesians 5:33 serves as a capstone in Paul's discourse on marital relationships, encapsulating what is expected from husbands in a single, yet powerful, directive: "Nevertheless, each one of you also must love his wife as he loves himself" (Ephesians 5:33, UASV).

The Context of Ephesians 5:33

A Continuation of Marital Guidance

The verse comes as a conclusion to an extended discussion on marriage that begins at Ephesians 5:22. While wives are instructed to be in subjection to their husbands, husbands are given the weighty responsibility of loving their wives with a sacrificial love.

The Gravity of the Command

It's worth noting that the Greek word for love used here is "agapao," indicating a selfless, sacrificial, unconditional love. It's the same kind of love with which Christ loved the church (Ephesians 5:25).

Obligations Enjoined Upon Husbands

Unconditional and Sacrificial Love

The obligation is unambiguous: Husbands must love their wives as they love themselves. This love is not based on the wife's performance, behavior, or any external circumstances; it's unconditional.

A Standard to Uphold: Christ's Love for the Church

Earlier in the same chapter, Paul uses the love of Christ for the church as a model for how husbands should love their wives. "Husbands, love your wives, just as Christ also loved the church and gave himself up for her" (Ephesians 5:25, UASV). This is *sacrificial love in its purest form* and serves as the standard a husband must strive to meet.

Emotional, Spiritual, and Physical Dimensions

The command to love one's wife as oneself inherently encompasses all aspects of a person's well-being—emotional, spiritual, and physical. It means to cherish her, to protect her, and to prioritize her needs above one's own.

Implications for the Marital Relationship

Foundation for Spiritual Leadership

A husband's love for his wife sets the foundation for his role as the spiritual leader in the family. He must guide her in truth, always using Scripture as the standard (2 Timothy 3:16-17).

Mutual Respect and Harmonious Living

The sacrificial love stipulated in Ephesians 5:33 fosters an environment of mutual respect. When a husband loves his wife in the manner commanded by Jehovah, it also makes it easier for the wife to fulfill her Scriptural role within the marriage (Ephesians 5:22-24).

The obligation imposed upon husbands in Ephesians 5:33 to love their wives as they love themselves is neither trivial nor optional. It serves as the cornerstone for a God-honoring marriage, reflecting Jehovah's original purpose for the marital arrangement. This command extends beyond mere affection; it is a call for enduring, sacrificial, and comprehensive love that finds its ultimate example in the love of Christ for His church.

Failure to Exercise Proper Headship: A Critical Examination for Husbands

The role of headship in marriage is a responsibility vested in husbands by the divine arrangement (1 Corinthians 11:3). While this position offers a unique opportunity to imitate Jehovah's love and righteousness, *some husbands fail to exercise this role properly, thereby misrepresenting divine principles and causing harm within the family structure.*

Misuse of Authority

Domineering Behavior

Some husbands mistake headship for authoritarian rule. This results in a domineering behavior that stifles the wife and inhibits her growth, both spiritually and emotionally. Paul specifically warns against this, urging husbands to love their wives as their own bodies (Ephesians 5:28-29).

Passive Aggressiveness

On the opposite end of the spectrum, some husbands manipulate their wives emotionally, using passive-aggressive tactics to exert their authority. This subverts the Scriptural principle of open and honest communication (Ephesians 4:25).

Negligence of Spiritual Leadership

Spiritual Apathy

A significant aspect of a husband's headship involves spiritual leadership. *Some husbands are spiritually lethargic, showing little interest in the family's spiritual well-being.* Such negligence opposes the Scriptural directive that a man must be the spiritual leader of his home (Joshua 24:15).

Unscriptural Decision-Making

Decisions that are not founded upon Scriptural principles but are instead based on worldly philosophies or convenience also represent a failure in exercising godly headship. The Word of God should be the ultimate authority in a Christian household (2 Timothy 3:16-17).

Financial Irresponsibility

Failure to Provide

1 Timothy 5:8 is unequivocal: "But if anyone does not provide for his own, and especially for those of his household, he has denied the faith and is worse than an

unbeliever." *Failure to provide materially for the family is a glaring omission in fulfilling the role of a husband.*

Excessive Control Over Finances

Conversely, some husbands may exert an unreasonable control over family finances, thereby neglecting the wife's Scriptural role as a "helper" in managing household affairs (Proverbs 31:10-31).

Emotional and Physical Negligence

Lack of Emotional Support

Headship also involves emotional and psychological well-being. *Failure to be a supportive partner in times of emotional need is a significant failing.* Peter advises husbands to dwell with their wives in understanding, granting her honor as a weaker vessel (1 Peter 3:7).

Physical Absence

Headship is not just a title; it requires an active presence. Some husbands neglect this by being physically absent from the family, making it impossible to exercise any form of godly leadership.

The failure to exercise proper headship in marriage is a disservice to the divine arrangement and can lead to disharmony and even spiritual danger for the family. Understanding the facets of this failure enables a husband to make the necessary corrections to align his role more closely with Scriptural directives, thereby glorifying Jehovah and enriching his marital relationship.

Decision-Making in the Family: Whose Views Should a Husband Consider?

The role of a husband in a Christian marriage is one of great responsibility, given that he is tasked with headship, akin to the role of Christ over the church (Ephesians 5:23). While this role certainly implies authority, it also comes with the requirement for *wisdom, humility, and consultative decision-making*.

The Wife's Perspective: A Valuable Asset

Recognizing the Role of the Wife as a Helper

In the divine arrangement, the wife is described as a "helper" (Genesis 2:18). In this capacity, she brings a unique set of skills, insights, and wisdom to the marriage. A wise husband acknowledges this and gives due weight to his wife's perspective when making decisions that affect the family.

Scriptural Mandate for Mutual Respect

The Bible calls for husbands to love their wives as their own bodies and respect them (Ephesians 5:28-33). *Consulting the wife in major family decisions is a practical way to demonstrate this love and respect.*

Consideration for Children

The Responsibility to Train and Nurture

Husbands and wives are given the charge to "train up a child in the way he should go" (Proverbs 22:6). If the

Edward D. Andrews

children are of an age where their input could be valuable, it may be beneficial for a husband to consider their views, especially on matters directly affecting them.

Moral and Spiritual Factors

Children in a Christian family are expected to "obey your parents in the Lord" (Ephesians 6:1). Yet, *obedience comes more readily when children feel that their views are considered and respected.*

Extended Family and Spiritual Community

Scriptural Balance of Responsibilities

While the immediate family takes precedence (1 Timothy 5:8), there may be occasions where the views of extended family and spiritual community could be relevant, particularly if they align with Scriptural principles. However, this should never supersede the immediate needs and considerations of the nuclear family.

God's Word: The Ultimate Guide

Conformity to Scriptural Principles

Above all, every decision must be weighed against the teachings of Scripture (2 Timothy 3:16-17). *The Word of God serves as the ultimate guide in any decision-making process.*

Prayerful Consideration

Before making any decision, a godly husband will approach Jehovah in prayer, asking for wisdom and guidance (James 1:5).

In sum, a Christian husband should take into account a diverse range of perspectives within the family and spiritual community when making decisions. *However, these should be weighted according to Scriptural directives, with the ultimate aim of glorifying Jehovah and fostering a harmonious family life.*

The Husband's Responsibility in Providing Material Necessities and the Role of Joint Effort

In a Christian marital framework, the husband holds a specific role that carries both authority and significant responsibilities. One of those responsibilities is the provision of the material necessities for the family. This discussion will focus on *what Scripture outlines concerning this role* and how, in reality, this often involves a *joint effort* between husband and wife.

The Husband's Scriptural Mandate to Provide Material Necessities

The Explicit Charge in 1 Timothy 5:8

The Apostle Paul underscores the importance of the husband's role as the provider in 1 Timothy 5:8: "But if anyone does not provide for his own, and especially for those of his household, he has denied the faith and is worse than an unbeliever." Here, the weight of this duty is made clear—failing in this responsibility is tantamount to denying one's Christian faith.

The Example of the "Ideal Husband" in Proverbs

The Old Testament also provides some insight into this role. Proverbs 31 describes a man who "sits in the gates," implying a sense of economic stability that he has secured for his family (Proverbs 31:23). While the main focus of this chapter is the ideal wife, it is understood that the husband's leadership contributes to the family's well-being.

The Role of Joint Effort in Providing Material Necessities

Scriptural Recognition of the Wife's Contribution

While the husband is explicitly tasked with the provision of material necessities, the Bible also recognizes the role of the wife in contributing to the family's economic well-being. The wife described in Proverbs 31 is an industrious woman whose efforts supplement the family income (Proverbs 31:13-24).

Partnership in Family Responsibilities

Scripturally, the wife is often seen as a "helper" to the husband (Genesis 2:18). In this role, she may assist in various ways to ensure the material well-being of the family. This can range from managing household finances prudently, to possibly working outside the home, if necessary and mutually agreed upon. *A wise husband acknowledges and appreciates his wife's contributions, understanding that their efforts are often complementary.*

Practical Implications: The Necessity of Communication and Planning

Open communication and joint planning are essential for successfully meeting the family's material needs. Both husband and wife need to discuss budgeting, expenses, and any financial goals. *This joint effort not only fulfills the immediate practical needs but also cultivates a spirit of unity and mutual respect.*

In summary, while the husband holds the primary responsibility for providing the material necessities of life as outlined in Scripture, *it is often by the joint efforts of both husband and wife that these provisions are effectively made.* Each brings unique abilities and insights to this joint endeavor, contributing to a more harmonious and fulfilling family life when aligned with Scriptural principles.

The Christian Perspective on Materialism in Marriage: Pitfalls to Avoid and the Ensuing Benefits

Materialism is a pervasive ideology that has permeated various aspects of our lives, including marriages. In a Christian context, the Bible offers clear guidelines on how married couples should view material possessions, reminding us that *earthly wealth is transitory* and should not be the focus of a God-centered marriage. Below we'll explore the *outlook to avoid* and the *benefits of adhering to Scriptural guidance* on materialism.

The Dangers of Materialism in Marriage

The Biblical Warnings

Scripture contains several stark warnings against materialism. One of the most direct comes from 1 Timothy 6:10, which states, "For the love of money is a root of all sorts of evil, and some by longing for it have wandered away from the faith and pierced themselves with many griefs." This text does not condemn money or material possessions themselves but emphasizes the danger of making them the focus of one's life.

Edward D. Andrews

The Pitfall of Covetousness

Another principle to be cautious of is covetousness. In the Ten Commandments, Jehovah tells us not to covet anything that belongs to our neighbor (Exodus 20:17). In a marriage, this might manifest as an unhealthy desire for a lifestyle or possessions seen in other couples, leading to unnecessary stress and strain in the relationship.

The Benefits of Avoiding a Materialistic Outlook

Fostering Spiritual Unity

By prioritizing spiritual goals over material ones, couples can grow in their relationship with Jehovah and with each other. Matthew 6:33 advises, "But seek first His kingdom and His righteousness, and all these things will be added to you." In a marriage, this translates to a mutual focus on spiritual activities like prayer, Bible study, and Christian ministry.

Financial Peace and Stability

Avoiding the trap of materialism can lead to better financial management. Proverbs 21:20 states, "There is precious treasure and oil in the dwelling of the wise, but a foolish man swallows it up." Wise financial stewardship can bring peace and stability to the home, eliminating one of the leading causes of marital discord.

Strengthening the Marital Bond

A mutual understanding that possessions are secondary to spiritual and relational health often leads to a stronger marital bond. This perspective minimizes conflicts over finances and fosters contentment, as stated in

Philippians 4:11-12, where Paul expresses his learned ability to be content in all financial situations.

The Christian view on materialism in marriage is clear: *it is an outlook to be avoided.* Couples should not make material possessions the focus of their union but should aim for a God-centered marriage. The benefits are manifold, including fostering spiritual unity, achieving financial peace, and ultimately strengthening the marital bond. Keeping in line with Scriptural guidance on this issue ensures that the couple sets a firm foundation not just for worldly success but for eternal rewards.

The Christian Perspective on Honoring One's Wife in Sexual Relations

Sexuality within a Christian marriage is a sacred topic, imbued with ethical considerations and implications for marital harmony. The Bible makes it clear that spouses are to honor each other in all aspects of marriage, including sexual relations. Below, let's delve into what the Bible teaches about *assigning "honor" to a wife* within the context of a sexual relationship in marriage and how that applies practically.

Biblical Foundation for Sexual Honor

The Imperative to Honor

The mandate to honor one's wife is not merely cultural or traditional but is Biblically grounded. The Apostle Peter instructs, "You husbands in the same way, live with your wives in an understanding way, as with someone weaker, since she is a woman; and show her honor as a fellow heir of the grace of life, so that your prayers will not be hindered" (1 Peter 3:7).

Sexuality within God's Design

In Hebrews 13:4, we are told, "Marriage is to be held in honor among all, and the marriage bed is to be undefiled; for fornicators and adulterers God will judge." This Scripture makes it clear that sexual relations within the bounds of marriage should be both honorable and undefiled.

Practical Ways to Honor One's Wife in Sexual Relations

Mutual Consent and Consideration

The Apostle Paul instructs married couples in 1 Corinthians 7:3-5 to not deprive each other, except by mutual consent and for a time to devote themselves to prayer. This principle underscores the idea that *both parties should be in agreement* regarding their sexual relationship.

Emotional Safety and Comfort

Assigning "honor" also entails ensuring emotional safety and comfort. This involves communicating openly about desires, boundaries, and any potential issues. A husband should be sensitive to his wife's emotional state, her needs, and her comfort level. This creates an environment of *trust* and *mutual respect*.

Prioritizing Her Needs

To honor one's wife in this area is to give attention to her sexual needs as well. This is aligned with the general Biblical principle of selflessness in marriage. Philippians 2:3-4 states, "Do nothing from selfishness or empty conceit, but with humility consider one another as more important than yourselves; do not merely look out for your own personal interests, but also for the interests of others."

Keeping the Marriage Bed Undefiled

This involves maintaining sexual purity, avoiding adultery, and abstaining from any sexual behaviors that would be considered morally or Scripturally unacceptable. In a way, keeping the marriage bed undefiled is an act of honoring not just your spouse but also Jehovah God.

Honoring one's wife in the context of sexual relations involves a multifaceted approach rooted in Biblical principles. It encompasses mutual consent, emotional safety, prioritization of her needs, and the preservation of the sanctity of the marital bond. Applying these principles contributes not just to a satisfying and respectful sexual relationship, but also to a deeper, more meaningful marital connection. This, in turn, helps to maintain a God-honoring marriage that stands as a testament to Jehovah's marvelous design for marital unity.

Gender Differences in Emotional Expression: A Biblical and Conservative Christian Perspective

Understanding the emotional differences between men and women can offer valuable insights for harmonious living, particularly in the context of Christian marriages and relationships. While it is important to avoid over-generalizing or stereotyping, some general patterns of emotional expression do appear to differ between the

45

genders. Below, we will explore these differences in light of Scripture and conservative Christian thought.

Biblical View on Emotional Design

Created in God's Image

Both men and women are made in the image of God (Genesis 1:27). This foundational belief affirms the inherent dignity and worth of each gender, including their emotional makeup. God's design includes specific emotional characteristics and proclivities for men and women.

Emotional Complexity in Scripture

Biblical characters display a range of emotions: David exhibited fear, joy, and sorrow; Esther showed courage; Hannah displayed sorrow and joy; Paul conveyed complex emotions like concern, love, and indignation. These examples show that emotional complexity is not confined to one gender.

General Emotional Differences between Men and Women

Emotional Expression

Women generally tend to be more expressive about their emotions. They often find comfort in sharing and talking through their feelings. This characteristic is reflected in the New Testament, where women like Mary and Martha openly express their grief and concern to Jesus (John 11:20-33).

Men, on the other hand, are often socialized to be more reserved about emotional expression, focusing more on problem-solving or action. In the Bible, men like Peter and Paul are often portrayed as direct and action-oriented, even in emotional situations (Acts 9:40, Philippians 1:12-14).

Emotional Intuition

Women are often considered to be more emotionally intuitive or empathic. This could be exemplified by the women at the tomb of Jesus who were sensitive to the profound loss and its implications (Matthew 28:1-8).

Men may often interpret emotional cues differently, focusing on tasks, challenges, or solutions. The Apostle Peter's desire to build shelters during the transfiguration of Jesus (Matthew 17:4) might be cited as an example of a task-oriented response to an emotional and spiritual experience.

Emotional Resilience and Coping

While men might be perceived as less emotionally expressive, they often manifest emotional resilience through action and problem-solving. For example, Joshua's reaction to challenges was often direct action, guided by his faith in Jehovah (Joshua 1:9).

Women may display emotional resilience through relational means, by seeking support and communal affirmation. Ruth's commitment to Naomi, even in the face of emotional loss and hardship, shows her resilience and the strength of relational bonds (Ruth 1:16-17).

Embracing Complementary Emotional Strengths

The Bible suggests that these emotional differences are not liabilities but rather complementary strengths that can be harmonized for God's glory. *Ephesians 5:21-33* provides the profound metaphor of marriage to describe the relationship between Christ and the church, illustrating that complementary roles can exist in unity and love.

In sum, while men and women may generally differ in how they process and express emotions, these differences are part of God's intricate design for humanity. Recognizing and appreciating these distinctions can lead to more harmonious relationships, stronger marriages, and communities more aligned with Scriptural principles.

The Importance of Communication and Giving in Marriage: A Scriptural Examination

The essence of a fruitful and harmonious Christian marriage rests on effective communication and the expression of love through giving. The Bible provides wisdom on how husbands can cultivate these vital aspects within the marital relationship. Below, we will delve into the significance of listening, talking, and gift-giving in the life of a Christian husband and what it means for his wife.

Listening and Talking: Foundations of a Godly Relationship

The Value of Active Listening

The Bible highlights the power and importance of the spoken word and its reception. *Proverbs 18:13* says, "He who gives an answer before he hears, that is folly and shame to him." Active listening is not just a modern psychological concept; it is a timeless Scriptural principle. When a husband genuinely listens to his wife, he follows a Christ-like example of compassion, empathy, and understanding.

Biblical Precedence for Open Communication

Ephesians 4:25 encourages believers to speak truthfully to their neighbors, for we are all members of one body. In the marital context, open communication is crucial. The narrative of Ananias and Sapphira in *Acts 5:1-11* serves as a sobering reminder of the catastrophic effects of dishonesty and lack of open dialogue between spouses.

How Listening and Talking Reflect Love and Respect

The apostle Peter tells husbands to dwell with their wives "in an understanding way" (*1 Peter 3:7*). "Understanding" in this context means not just intellectually grasping a point, but understanding through active engagement and dialogue. In doing so, husbands emulate Christ's loving and sacrificial relationship with the church (*Ephesians 5:25-30*).

The Message Behind Gifts: Tangible Acts of Love

The Significance of Gift-Giving

Gifts serve as an external symbol of internal affection and attention. Giving gifts is not just a cultural practice but a Scriptural one. The Wise Men offered gifts to the baby Jesus as an act of homage and respect (*Matthew 2:11*). Similarly, a husband's gift to his wife can be a tangible expression of his love, respect, and appreciation.

What Kind of Giving is Most Important?

While material gifts have their place, the most impactful giving comes from the heart—a giving of time, attention, and emotional support. The Bible says that "a cheerful heart is good medicine" (*Proverbs 17:22*). Emotional and spiritual support often supersedes the value of material gifts.

In *Ephesians 5:28*, Paul notes, "In the same way husbands should love their wives as their own bodies." This is not just a physical provision but includes emotional and spiritual nurturing, which could be viewed as a continuous gift to one's spouse.

The Balanced Role of Communication and Giving in a Christian Marriage

In summary, a balanced Christian marriage is nurtured through the active processes of listening and talking, as well as through tangible and intangible acts of giving. These are not mere societal constructs but are rooted in biblical principles that reflect the heart of God towards His creation.

A husband's willingness to listen to his wife, communicate openly, and give selflessly are not just marital duties; they are spiritual acts of worship that reflect the love of Christ. By doing so, husbands not only enrich their marital relationships but also fulfill God's design for a loving, godly marriage.

Self-Examination for Proper Exercise of Headship: A Scriptural Guide

Understanding the gravity and responsibility of headship in a marriage relationship is crucial for any

Christian husband. With the wisdom imparted through Scripture, it becomes possible for men to continuously assess their role and make improvements where necessary. This reflective process is not only beneficial for the family but is a crucial aspect of walking in obedience to God's Word.

Key Questions for Self-Examination

Am I Following Christ's Example?

A husband must first ask himself if he is following the example of Christ, who is the head of the Church. The apostle Paul instructs, "Husbands, love your wives, just as Christ loved the church and gave Himself up for her" (*Ephesians 5:25*). In this statement, Paul sets a high bar for husbands: the sacrificial love exhibited by Christ Himself.

Do I Lead with Humility and Love?

It's vital to assess whether your leadership style reflects humility and love or if it veers towards authoritarianism or negligence. *Philippians 2:3* says, "Do nothing from selfish ambition or conceit, but in humility count others more significant than yourselves." If a husband's motives for leadership are rooted in self-interest or ego, he misses the biblical model of headship.

Am I Providing for My Family's Needs?

1 Timothy 5:8 cautions, "But if anyone does not provide for his own, and especially for those of his household, he has denied the faith and is worse than an unbeliever." Provision here is comprehensive—spiritual, emotional, and material. Are you taking steps to ensure your family's comprehensive well-being?

Am I Listening to My Wife?

51

Edward D. Andrews

As touched upon in *1 Peter 3:7*, husbands are instructed to live with their wives "in an understanding way." This involves not just speaking but actively listening to the concerns, dreams, and wisdom that the wife brings into the family dynamic.

How Well Am I Balancing Authority and Autonomy?

The headship role does not negate the individuality and agency of the wife. *Galatians 3:28* reminds us that "There is neither Jew nor Greek, there is neither slave nor free, there is no male and female, for you are all one in Christ Jesus." Are you honoring your wife's individuality and incorporating her insights into family decisions?

The Importance of This Self-Examination

Maintaining Scriptural Integrity

Regular self-examination ensures that a husband is aligning his role with the biblical mandate for headship, thereby pleasing God and becoming a more effective leader within his home.

Fostering Spiritual Growth

Self-examination is a catalyst for spiritual growth. As *2 Corinthians 13:5* advises, "Examine yourselves, to see whether you are in the faith. Test yourselves."

Enhancing Family Harmony

A husband who consistently checks his style and methods of leadership against the backdrop of Scriptural teachings contributes to a more harmonious, loving, and spiritually robust family environment.

The Necessity of Self-Examination in Righteous Headship

In conclusion, a husband's routine self-examination to ensure he is aligning with biblical principles is not just advisable; it is a Scriptural imperative. It aligns the family structure with God's designed order, fosters spiritual growth, and contributes to a more loving and harmonious household. Thus, being concerned about proper headship is not just good; it is a requisite for fulfilling God's plan for marriage.

CHAPTER 3 Two Keys to a Lasting Marriage

The Design and Duration of Marriage: A Scriptural Examination

Marriage is not just a human institution; it's a divine design with a prescribed order and objective. Understanding how long marriage was intended to last and how two individuals can maintain a joyous union for an extended period is vital for upholding this sacred covenant in the way God intended.

Marriage: Designed to Last a Lifetime

Marriage as a Permanent Union: *Genesis 2:24* establishes the foundational principle that "a man shall leave his father and his mother, and shall cleave unto his wife: and they shall be one flesh." The verb "cleave" implies a permanent, unbreakable bond. It's a one-flesh relationship, which signifies unity and permanence.

The Warning Against Divorce: In *Matthew 19:6*, Jesus reinforces the original intention for marriage by stating, "So they are no longer two, but one flesh. What therefore God has joined together, let no man separate." Jesus elaborates on the circumstances under which divorce was permitted but underscores that it was not the original intent (*Matthew 19:8*).

Death as the Termination Point: According to *Romans 7:2–3*, the marriage covenant naturally ends when one of the spouses dies. It states, "For the married woman is bound by law to her husband while he is living; but if her husband dies, she is released from the law concerning the husband."

The Keys to Long-Lasting Happiness in Marriage

Spiritual Foundation

A strong spiritual foundation is the cornerstone of a long-lasting, happy marriage. *Ecclesiastes 4:12* states, "And if one can overpower him who is alone, two can resist him. A cord of three strands is not quickly torn apart." In a Christian marriage, those three strands are the husband, the wife, and God.

Open and Honest Communication

The Apostle Paul's words in *Ephesians 4:25-27* apply well to marriage: "Therefore, laying aside falsehood, speak truth each one of you with his neighbor, for we are members of one another." Open and honest communication prevents misunderstandings and builds trust.

Self-Sacrificial Love

The love described in *1 Corinthians 13:4-7* is a selfless, sacrificial love. It's a love that "bears all things, believes all things, hopes all things, endures all things." This is the love that both spouses should strive for, taking their cue from Christ's love for the Church (*Ephesians 5:25*).

Mutual Respect

The Bible tells husbands to show honor to their wives and treat them with understanding (*1 Peter 3:7*), while wives are encouraged to respect their husbands (*Ephesians 5:33*). Mutual respect nurtures love and unity.

Adaptability and Forgiveness

Couples will face challenges, but adapting to each other's needs and forgiving each other's shortcomings are critical for long-term happiness. The Bible urges us to "Be kind to one another, tender-hearted, forgiving each other, just as God in Christ also has forgiven you" (*Ephesians 4:32*).

Eternal Principles for Temporal Bliss

Marriage, according to the divine blueprint, is designed to last a lifetime, ending only with the death of one of the spouses. By adhering to spiritual principles such as a strong spiritual foundation, open and honest communication, self-sacrificial love, mutual respect, adaptability, and forgiveness, it is more than possible for two individuals to live together in a harmonious, lasting relationship. These principles are not just the secret to temporal happiness but are deeply rooted in God's eternal truths.

The First Key

The Threefold Love in Marriage: A Scriptural Framework

The institution of marriage is not merely a social contract; it is a divine covenant. A successful marriage does not run on a single type of love but requires a multifaceted approach to cultivate various forms of love. According to Scripture, there are three essential kinds of love that should be nurtured by marriage mates: Agape, Phileo, and Eros.

Agape Love: Unconditional, Self-Sacrificial Love

Biblical Basis

The highest form of love is Agape love, which is unconditional and self-sacrificial. This type of love is the one most prominently featured in the New Testament, especially in relation to God's love for us. It is also the love that spouses are to have for one another.

Key Scripture: *Ephesians 5:25* specifically instructs husbands to "love your wives, just as Christ also loved the church and gave Himself up for her." The word "love" used here is "agape," signifying a love that seeks the best for the other person, without expecting anything in return.

Practical Application

Agape love means prioritizing the needs of your spouse above your own needs. It is love in action—serving one another, showing kindness, and making sacrifices. The application of this love is not dependent on emotion or circumstance; it is a committed act of the will.

Phileo Love: Brotherly Love, Friendship

Biblical Basis

The second type of love that should be cultivated in a marriage is Phileo love, often translated as "brotherly love" or "friendship." The word is used in *Titus 2:4*, where the older women are instructed to encourage the young women "to love their husbands."

Key Scripture: One verse that signifies the importance of Phileo love is *Song of Solomon 5:16*, where the bride describes her spouse as "my beloved and my friend." Though the original language is Hebrew, the sentiment perfectly embodies what Phileo love is all about.

Practical Application

Phileo love encompasses the relational aspects of marriage—the companionship, the shared interests, and the mutual respect that binds a couple together. It is the type of love that results in a deep emotional connection, enriching the marital relationship.

Eros Love: Romantic, Sexual Love

Biblical Basis

Eros, or the romantic and sexual love between a husband and a wife, is not explicitly named in the Bible but is clearly a God-designed component of marital love.

Key Scripture: The *Song of Solomon* is an entire book dedicated to the passionate and romantic love between a husband and a wife. For instance, *Song of Solomon 7:10* states, "I am my beloved's, and his desire is for me."

Practical Application

Eros love includes physical attraction and intimacy, which are essential components of a marriage relationship. This love needs to be cultivated and protected within the bounds of marriage. It is not merely a physical act but an emotional and spiritual bonding between a husband and a wife.

A Balanced Marriage is a Threefold Cord

A thriving marriage requires all three types of love. Agape love lays the foundation for self-sacrifice and unconditional commitment; Phileo love strengthens friendship and companionship; Eros love adds the vital elements of physical attraction and intimacy. Each of these loves serves a unique role in creating a resilient, fulfilling marriage relationship. It is only when all three are present and actively cultivated that a marriage truly reflects the divine design. *Ecclesiastes 4:12* says, "A cord of three strands is not quickly torn apart," which can aptly apply to the three kinds of love that strengthen the marital bond.

The Supremacy of Love in Marriage: A Biblical Examination

The Apostle Paul, in his first letter to the Corinthians, gives us an incredible treatise on love, famously stating, "And now these three remain: faith, hope, and love. But the greatest of these is love" (*1 Corinthians 13:13*). Paul's discourse is not just poetic but deeply theological and profoundly practical, especially when applied to marriage. Here, we will unpack why love is considered the greatest and how it contributes to the longevity of a marital relationship.

Theological Foundations: Why Love is Greater Than Faith and Hope

Biblical Basis

While faith is the conviction of things unseen and the assurance of our salvation (*Hebrews 11:1*), and hope is the expectation of our future glory with Christ (*Romans 5:2*), love stands supreme for several reasons.

Key Scripture: *1 John 4:16* reads, "So we have come to know and to believe the love that God has for us. God is love, and whoever abides in love abides in God, and God abides in him."

Immutable Nature of God's Love

Firstly, love is part of the immutable nature of God. God *is* love. While faith and hope are qualities that depend on an object or an outcome, love is an intrinsic attribute of God's character. Because we are created in the image of God, the highest expression of our godliness is love.

Eternal Continuance

Secondly, love is eternal. Faith and hope are time-bound; they are needed for this earthly life and will find their fulfillment in heaven. In contrast, love will continue for eternity. *Romans 8:38-39* assures us that nothing can separate us from the love of God, indicating its eternal nature.

The Fulfillment of the Law

Thirdly, love is the fulfillment of the Law. In *Romans 13:10*, Paul states, "Love does no wrong to a neighbor; therefore love is the fulfilling of the law." Whereas faith and hope are virtues that primarily concern our relationship with God, love has a horizontal aspect, affecting our relationships with others.

Practical Implications: Love as the Cornerstone of a Lasting Marriage

Emotional Security

One of the foundational reasons why love helps make a marriage last is the emotional security it provides. *Ephesians 5:25-28* outlines how a husband should love his wife as Christ loved the Church. This sets a high standard, one of selfless sacrifice and unconditional love, providing emotional security and trust within the marriage.

Conflict Resolution

Conflicts are inevitable in marriage. However, love, when it is the kind described in *1 Corinthians 13:4-7*—patient, kind, not envious, and not easily angered—becomes the ultimate tool for conflict resolution. When spouses truly love each other, they are motivated to resolve issues for the benefit of both parties.

Mutual Growth and Flourishing

The Bible says in *Proverbs 27:17*, "Iron sharpens iron, and one man sharpens another." In a marriage filled with love, both spouses encourage each other to grow spiritually, emotionally, and even intellectually. Love seeks the best for the other person, leading to mutual edification and lifelong flourishing.

Creates a Legacy of Faith

When children see a marriage rooted in love, they are more likely to emulate those same qualities. A loving marriage thus becomes a powerful testimony and a means of generational blessing. *Deuteronomy 6:5-7* speaks to the power of teaching the next generation, and nothing teaches better than a lived example.

Fosters Resilience

In times of trials and tribulations, it's love that carries the relationship through. Love fosters resilience because it bears all things, believes all things, hopes all things, endures all things (*1 Corinthians 13:7*).

Love as the Lifeblood of Marriage

Love, as defined and modeled by God, is the lifeblood of a successful, lasting marriage. It goes beyond the superficial to address the deepest emotional, spiritual, and even physical needs of both parties. It has both a vertical relationship with God and a horizontal relationship with our spouse. A marriage built on love is not just an earthly contract but a heavenly covenant, designed to last "until death do us part" (*Romans 7:2*).

The Second Key

The Role of Respect in a Biblical Marriage

The concept of respect is essential in understanding the dynamics of a biblical marriage. The Bible makes it clear that both spouses have a role to play in maintaining a relationship of mutual respect. Let's explore the dimensions of respect, its biblical injunctions, and how respect contributes to a stable and happy marital relationship.

Defining Respect: What It Is and What It Isn't

Key Scripture: *Ephesians 5:33* states, "However, let each one of you love his wife as himself, and let the wife see that she respects her husband."

Conceptual Clarification

Respect is a multifaceted concept that goes beyond mere courtesy or superficial politeness. It encompasses a deep regard for the person's inherent worth, as well as their thoughts, feelings, and wishes. Respect is not subservience, nor is it an acceptance of harmful or abusive behavior.

Biblical Directives: Who Should Show Respect?

The Wife's Role

According to *Ephesians 5:22-24*, wives are instructed to submit to their husbands as unto the Lord. This submission is a form of respect but should never be misconstrued as inferiority. The respect a wife shows her husband is an acknowledgment of the headship that God has instituted in the marriage relationship.

The Husband's Role

The Bible does not let husbands off the hook. While the term "respect" might not be explicitly mentioned for husbands, the call for men to love their wives as Christ loved the Church (*Ephesians 5:25*) carries a deeply respectful connotation. This love is sacrificial and considers the wife's needs, opinions, and feelings, thereby embodying a form of highest respect.

Practical Applications: How Respect Stabilizes and Enriches Marriage

Mutual Trust

One of the primary ways that respect enhances a marital relationship is by fostering mutual trust. When spouses respect each other's boundaries, choices, and independent thinking, it builds a sense of safety and trust (*Proverbs 31:11*).

Effective Communication

Respect is a cornerstone of effective communication. When spouses listen to each other's viewpoints without demeaning or belittling, they create an atmosphere for open dialogue and resolution of conflicts (*James 1:19*).

Emotional Well-being

Being respected by one's spouse significantly contributes to one's emotional well-being. This emotional stability can be a buffer against external stressors and challenges that a couple may face (*Philippians 2:3-4*).

Spiritual Unity

When both spouses respect each other, they are more likely to be in unity concerning spiritual matters. This spiritual unity can be a great source of strength for the marriage (*Amos 3:3*).

Upholding Dignity

Showing respect ensures that the inherent dignity of your spouse is upheld. It is an affirmation of the image of God in them, according to *Genesis 1:27*.

Creating a Legacy

Finally, a respectful marriage sets a positive example for children and others who observe the relationship, thereby creating a lasting legacy (*Deuteronomy 6:5-7*).

The Imperative of Respect

Respect is not optional in a Christian marriage; it is imperative. Both the husband and wife have unique roles in showing respect to each other, as outlined by Scripture. This mutual respect forms the backbone of a stable and joyous marriage, ensuring not just its survival but its thriving for the glory of God.

The Vital Role of Communication in a Christian Marriage

The topic of communication is crucial for understanding the biblical portrait of marriage. God instituted marriage as a union where two become one flesh (*Genesis 2:24*), and to maintain this unity, love and respect must be regularly communicated. This article will delve into why communication is vital, how proper speech contributes to marital happiness, and the necessary attitudes for maintaining good communication.

The Importance of Communication: Where Love and Respect Intersect

Key Scriptures: *Ephesians 4:29*; *Colossians 4:6*

The Channel for Love and Respect

Love and respect are not just felt; they are communicated. Whether it's a husband lovingly listening to his wife's concerns or a wife respectfully voicing her own opinions, effective communication is the conduit through which these virtues flow.

Emotional and Spiritual Intimacy

Without good communication, emotional and spiritual intimacy suffer. Communication allows for the exchange of thoughts, beliefs, and emotions, making it the fabric that knits souls together.

Problem-Solving and Conflict Resolution

Edward D. Andrews

Every marriage faces challenges. How these are communicated about often determines whether conflicts strengthen the marital bond or weaken it. Love and respect are essential in these dialogues to ensure both parties feel heard and valued (*Matthew 18:15-17*).

Proper Speech: The Building Block of a Happy Marriage

Key Scriptures: *Proverbs 15:1*, *Ephesians 4:15*

Words That Build Up

Ephesians 4:29 advises, "Let no corrupting talk come out of your mouths, but only such as is good for building up, as fits the occasion, that it may give grace to those who hear." This advice is particularly crucial in marriage, where words have the power to build up or tear down.

Honesty Coupled with Tact

While honesty is essential, how something is said is often as important as what is said. Speaking the truth in love (*Ephesians 4:15*) is a skill that couples must cultivate.

Encouragement and Praise

Regularly expressing affirmation and admiration can solidify the marital bond and create an atmosphere of goodwill (*1 Thessalonians 5:11*).

Essential Attitudes for Good Communication

Humility

Humility allows us to admit when we are wrong and to listen to our spouse's perspective without becoming defensive (*Philippians 2:3-4*).

Patience

Quick responses can often escalate conflicts. Patience helps us to listen more and speak less, providing room for more thoughtful communication (*James 1:19*).

Forgiveness

Keeping short accounts and being willing to forgive ensures that communication lines remain open and free from the blockage of lingering bitterness (*Colossians 3:13*).

Communication as the Lifeline of Marriage

A Christian marriage cannot thrive without love and respect, and these virtues cannot be sustained without effective communication. Proper speech and the right attitudes towards communication will not only solve problems but also deepen the emotional and spiritual intimacy between a husband and wife. It is an indispensable component that serves to edify both individuals within the marriage while glorifying God.

The Role of Love and Respect in Handling Marital Disagreements

Navigating through disagreements is an inevitable part of any marriage. However, Scripture provides enduring principles that, when applied, can turn these potentially divisive situations into opportunities for growth and unity. The twin pillars that can uphold a marriage during these times are love and respect.

The Biblical Mandate for Love and Respect

Key Scriptures: *Ephesians 5:25, 33*; *1 Peter 3:7*

The apostle Paul in *Ephesians 5:25* instructs husbands to love their wives as Christ loved the church. This agape love is selfless, sacrificial, and unconditional. In the same chapter, both husbands and wives are told to give respect and love (*Ephesians 5:33*). Peter also emphasizes that husbands should honor their wives as weaker vessels and heirs together of the grace of life (*1 Peter 3:7*).

Love Breaks Down Barriers

When disagreements arise, showing unconditional love can help in breaking down emotional barriers. A husband or wife wrapped in a protective layer of pride or anger may soften when met with genuine love.

Respect Builds Bridges

When a spouse feels respected, they are more likely to be open to understanding their partner's viewpoint. Showing respect can mean listening actively and refraining from interruptive or disrespectful behavior during a disagreement.

Examples of Love and Respect in Action During Disagreements

Example 1: Financial Decisions

Suppose a husband wants to invest in a risky business venture while his wife prefers a safer financial approach. Here, love and respect manifest as follows:

- The husband, **loving his wife**, might willingly and attentively listen to her concerns, valuing her input as an equal partner in the decision-making process.

- The wife, **respecting her husband**, would present her viewpoint without demeaning his judgment or decision-making abilities.

Example 2: Parenting Discrepancies

Assume the wife believes in disciplining their children differently than her husband.

- She expresses her **love** by being sensitive to his feelings, emphasizing that her different approach isn't a critique of his parenting but rather a complementary strategy.

- He shows **respect** by not dismissing her ideas outright, instead engaging in an open dialogue to find a middle ground.

Example 3: Choices About Leisure Time

A husband wants to go fishing every weekend, but the wife feels they should spend more time together as a family.

- **Love** from the husband could manifest in his willingness to compromise on the frequency of his fishing trips.

- **Respect** from the wife may show in her acknowledgement that he needs some time to engage in activities that bring him joy, without criticizing him for it.

Edward D. Andrews

Why Love and Respect are Indispensable During Disagreements

Fosters Emotional Safety

A marriage marked by love and respect becomes a safe space where both parties feel emotionally secure enough to express disagreements without fear of ridicule or condemnation.

Promotes Constructive Dialogue

When love and respect are the norms, disagreements turn into constructive dialogues rather than destructive arguments. Both parties focus more on finding solutions rather than winning an argument.

Reinforces the Marital Bond

Successfully navigating through disagreements by applying love and respect fortifies the marital bond and serves as a testimony to the indomitable strength of a God-honoring union.

The Transformative Power of Love and Respect

When applied earnestly, love and respect have the power to transform potentially divisive disagreements into opportunities for growth, deepening intimacy, and greater unity in marriage. Following the Biblical guidelines can help couples tackle any issue that arises, to the glory of God and the strengthening of their marital union.

The Role of God's Word in Sustaining Marital Happiness Through Ups and Downs

Every marriage experiences peaks and valleys—times of joy and hardship, closeness and distance. It's the natural cycle of any long-term relationship. Yet, God's Word serves as an unfailing guide that can steer a marital relationship toward happiness and fulfillment, even during trying times. Let's explore how Scripture accomplishes this vital role.

The Authority and Sufficiency of Scripture for Marriage

Key Scriptures: *2 Timothy 3:16-17; Psalm 19:7-11*

The Apostle Paul states in *2 Timothy 3:16-17* that all Scripture is inspired by God and is profitable for teaching, reproof, correction, and training in righteousness so that the man of God may be fully equipped for every good work. Marriage, being a good work instituted by God (*Genesis 2:24*), falls under this provision. *Psalm 19:7-11* also extols the perfection and sufficiency of God's law, stating that it revives the soul and makes wise the simple.

Navigational Guide through Marital Challenges

Scripture acts as a compass during times of difficulty, providing wisdom and moral grounding. It contains the principles that can resolve conflict, foster love, and nurture respect between spouses.

Source of Consistent Principles

Marriage is an evolving relationship, but the principles laid down in Scripture are unchanging. They provide a stable foundation on which to build marital happiness, irrespective of changing circumstances.

Practical Ways God's Word Helps in Marital Happiness

Encourages Mutual Respect and Love

Ephesians 5:25, 33 clearly instructs husbands and wives on the roles of love and respect. These roles are symbiotic and complementary, helping to foster a joyful marital environment.

Enhances Communication

James 1:19 encourages us to be "quick to listen, slow to speak, slow to anger," a principle that if applied, can revolutionize marital communication.

Enables Conflict Resolution

The model of forgiveness and reconciliation laid down by Christ (*Matthew 18:21-22*; *Ephesians 4:32*) provides a framework for resolving disagreements in a healthy and constructive manner.

Provides a Framework for Sexual Intimacy

Hebrews 13:4 emphasizes the holiness and exclusivity of the marital bed, framing sexual relations as both joyful and sacred.

Cultivates Patience and Longsuffering

1 Corinthians 13:4-7 offers an exhaustive definition of love that includes patience and longsuffering. This is particularly useful for maintaining happiness even in the midst of challenges.

Why God's Word is Essential for Marital Stability and Happiness

Infuses Divine Wisdom

Scripture connects us to the mind of God, imparting wisdom that is far above human understanding (*Proverbs 2:6*).

Facilitates Spiritual Growth

As both spouses grow in their understanding and application of Scripture, they also grow spiritually. This spiritual growth has a positive ripple effect on the marital relationship.

Strengthens the Marital Bond

By offering a higher purpose—serving God—Scripture enhances the marital bond. The unity found in joint spiritual pursuit can be deeply stabilizing and joy-inducing (*Amos 3:3*).

The Lasting Impact of God's Word on Marital Happiness

Listening to and applying God's Word can provide the wisdom, direction, and sustenance needed for a lasting, happy marriage. As couples commit to aligning their marriage with Scriptural principles, they will find that even in the ups and downs, there is a bedrock of joy, respect, and love that cannot be easily shaken. Therefore, it is not merely advisable but essential for couples to diligently apply the teachings of Scripture to their marital life.

Edward D. Andrews

CHAPTER 4 Build a Strong and Happy Marriage

Challenges in Building a Strong and Happy Marriage

Marriage is a divine institution, designed by God as a lifelong union between a man and a woman (*Genesis 2:24*). Despite its divine origin, marriage requires consistent work and is often beset with challenges. Understanding these challenges is crucial for navigating the complexities of marital life effectively. Here are some common challenges along with scriptural insights on how to tackle them.

Financial Stress

Key Scriptures: *Proverbs 22:7*, *1 Timothy 6:10*

One of the most common causes of marital tension is financial stress. Whether it is debt, differing spending habits, or income disparities, money issues can wreak havoc in a marriage. The Scripture warns that "the borrower is a slave to the lender" (*Proverbs 22:7*) and that "the love of money is a root of all kinds of evil" (*1 Timothy 6:10*).

Navigating the Challenge:

Clear, honest communication about financial expectations and budgeting can go a long way. Prayerful consideration and mutual agreement on financial priorities are essential.

Communication Breakdown

Key Scriptures: *James 1:19, Ephesians 4:29*

Communication is vital for the health of any marriage. Failure to communicate effectively can lead to misunderstandings, resentments, and emotional disconnection. *James 1:19* urges us to be "quick to listen, slow to speak, slow to anger."

Navigating the Challenge:

Both parties must make a conscious effort to listen actively and speak honestly yet respectfully. The counsel in *Ephesians 4:29* to let no corrupting talk come out of your mouths can be particularly helpful here.

Conflicting Roles and Expectations

Key Scriptures: *Ephesians 5:22-33, 1 Peter 3:1-7*

Society often imposes its own roles and expectations on a married couple, which can conflict with the Biblical model. The Bible gives specific roles to husbands and wives (*Ephesians 5:22-33; 1 Peter 3:1-7*), yet these are often misunderstood or ignored.

Navigating the Challenge:

Couples should seek to understand and apply Biblical roles and responsibilities, respecting the divinely instituted hierarchy while cherishing mutual respect and love.

Edward D. Andrews

Sexual Incompatibility and Temptations

Key Scriptures: *1 Corinthians 7:3-5*, *Hebrews 13:4*

Sexual issues are another common challenge. These can range from differing libidos to struggles with sexual sin. The Bible is clear that the marital bed should be kept pure (*Hebrews 13:4*), and that spouses should not deprive one another (*1 Corinthians 7:3-5*).

Navigating the Challenge:

Open and honest communication is essential. Both partners should work on being sensitive to each other's needs and setting healthy boundaries to protect their marital purity.

Emotional and Psychological Challenges

Key Scriptures: *Galatians 5:22-23*, *Philippians 4:6-7*

Emotions play a significant role in marital happiness. Emotional neglect, psychological issues, or the lack of emotional intelligence can pose serious challenges. The fruit of the Spirit (*Galatians 5:22-23*) is essential for emotional well-being, and *Philippians 4:6-7* gives us the peace that transcends all understanding.

Navigating the Challenge:

Both spouses should strive to be emotionally supportive and consider seeking Christian counseling for persistent issues.

The Necessity of Christ-Centered Resilience

Marriage is not for the faint of heart. Yet, it remains one of the most rewarding relationships that humans can experience. To build a strong and happy marriage, couples must recognize the challenges they will face and be prepared to tackle them with wisdom, commitment, and the application of Scriptural principles. This Christ-centered resilience will not only help overcome challenges but also will deepen the marital bond.

Including God in Building a Strong and Happy Marriage

Incorporating God into the marital relationship is not just an option; it is essential for any Christian couple aspiring to have a strong and enduring marriage. Since marriage was instituted by God, including Him in the marriage means aligning your marital goals, values, and practices with His design and will. Let's explore how a couple can intentionally involve God in their marital life.

Prioritize Prayer

Key Scriptures: *Matthew 18:19-20, 1 Thessalonians 5:17*

Prayer is not merely a religious obligation but a powerful means of invoking divine assistance and guidance. Jesus promises that "where two or three are gathered in my name, there am I among them" (*Matthew 18:20*). Daily praying together not only fosters unity but also invites God's presence into your home and relationship.

Practical Application:

Set aside specific times for communal prayer and ensure you cover various aspects of your marriage, including current challenges, in your petitions.

Edward D. Andrews

Study Scripture Together

Key Scriptures: *2 Timothy 3:16-17, Psalm 119:105*

The Word of God is "profitable for teaching, for reproof, for correction, and for training in righteousness" (*2 Timothy 3:16*). Studying the Scriptures together provides you both with the moral and ethical framework upon which to base your lives and marriage.

Practical Application:

Regular Bible study sessions should be a fixture in your marriage. Delve into passages about marriage, familial responsibilities, love, and forgiveness, applying these teachings in your daily lives.

Implement Biblical Roles

Key Scriptures: *Ephesians 5:22-33, Colossians 3:18-19*

The Bible provides role-specific guidelines for husbands and wives. Understanding and implementing these roles under the lordship of Christ can significantly benefit your marriage. For instance, Ephesians 5 outlines the leadership role of the husband and the supportive role of the wife, all modeled after Christ's relationship with the church.

Practical Application:

Husbands must love their wives "as Christ loved the church" (*Ephesians 5:25*), while wives are called to submit "as to the Lord" (*Ephesians 5:22*). These roles should be understood and exercised not as cultural constructs but as God-ordained pathways to marital harmony.

Foster a Spirit-led Life

Key Scriptures: *Galatians 5:22-23, Romans 8:5-6*

While the indwelling of the Holy Spirit may not be accepted by all, His role through the inspired Word is pivotal for a Christian's life. Galatians 5 describes the fruit of the Spirit—attributes such as love, joy, and peace—that should permeate your character and consequently your marriage.

Practical Application:

Make a conscious effort to apply the fruit of the Spirit in your interactions with your spouse. Live by the Spirit's guidelines as outlined in Scripture, setting your minds on what the Spirit desires (*Romans 8:5*).

Worship and Fellowship

Key Scriptures: *Hebrews 10:25, Matthew 18:20*

Engaging in corporate worship and fellowship with other believers has a communal effect that can fortify your marriage. Hebrews 10:25 advises us not to forsake meeting together, as it is a means of mutual encouragement.

Practical Application:

Regular church attendance, involvement in a couples' ministry, or joining a small group can provide additional layers of accountability and support. It serves as a weekly re-centering around Christ's teachings and a reminder of your spiritual commitments.

A Threefold Cord

Edward D. Andrews

Ecclesiastes 4:12 observes that "a threefold cord is not quickly broken." A marriage that involves the couple and God forms this formidable threefold cord. Making God an integral part of your marriage does not guarantee the absence of problems, but it assures you of a reservoir of wisdom, strength, and grace to navigate whatever challenges may come your way. By implementing these practical, Scripture-based steps, couples set a course toward a marriage that glorifies God and edifies both spouses.

Applying the Golden Rule in Marriage

The Golden Rule, "Do to others as you would have them do to you," is found in the Sermon on the Mount (*Matthew 7:12*). This maxim is a staple in ethical and moral reasoning and has particular relevance in marital relationships. By applying the Golden Rule, couples not only build a strong marital bond but also create an environment conducive to happiness and growth. Here's how:

Mutual Respect

Key Scriptures: *Ephesians 5:33, 1 Peter 3:7*

Respect is a foundational aspect of any relationship, and more so in marriage. Paul emphasizes that each one of you must "respect his wife" (*Ephesians 5:33*) and Peter talks about treating your wives "with respect" (*1 Peter 3:7*). Applying the Golden Rule in this context means respecting your spouse in the way you desire to be respected.

Practical Application:

Be mindful of your tone, words, and actions. Show appreciation and recognize the worth and contributions of your spouse, just as you would want to be appreciated and recognized.

Effective Communication

Key Scriptures: *James 1:19-20, Proverbs 15:1*

The Bible advises us to be "quick to hear, slow to speak, slow to anger" (*James 1:19*). This is crucial in marital communication. To apply the Golden Rule, one should listen to their spouse in the same manner they wish to be listened to.

Practical Application:

Be an active listener when your spouse speaks. Refrain from interrupting and give feedback that indicates you understand, or seek clarification if you do not.

Emotional and Physical Intimacy

Key Scriptures: *1 Corinthians 7:3-5, Song of Solomon 4:9-10*

Physical and emotional intimacy should be consensual and reciprocal. Paul instructs that spouses should fulfill their marital duties to each other (*1 Corinthians 7:3-5*). This principle could be extended to emotional needs as well.

Practical Application:

Engage in physical affection and emotional sharing in a manner you wish your spouse to be physically and emotionally available to you.

Financial Stewardship

Key Scriptures: *Proverbs 3:9-10, 1 Timothy 5:8*

Financial decisions in a family impact both partners. Applying the Golden Rule means treating the family's resources with the same responsibility and caution as you would want your spouse to exercise.

Practical Application:

Before making major financial decisions, consult your spouse and come to a mutual agreement. Practice transparency in your financial dealings.

Conflict Resolution

Key Scriptures: *Ephesians 4:26-27, Matthew 18:15-17*

Disagreements are natural in any relationship. The Bible advises us to resolve conflicts without letting the sun go down on our anger (*Ephesians 4:26*). The Golden Rule's application here would be to approach conflict resolution in the way you'd want your spouse to approach it with you.

Practical Application:

Address issues head-on but with tact, avoiding blame. Strive for solutions that are fair and mutually beneficial. Always confirm your mutual understanding to resolve the issue.

The Golden Rule as a Marital Compass

Incorporating the Golden Rule into marriage serves as an ethical and moral compass guiding actions and decisions. It engenders a cycle of good will and positive behavior between spouses. It echoes Christ's selfless love and service, raising the quality of marital interaction to a divine standard. Thus, by "doing to others"—in this case, your spouse—"what you would have them do to you," you establish a powerful and lasting marital bond.

Edward D. Andrews

CHAPTER 5 Making Christian Marriage a Success

Responsibilities in Christian Marriage: God's Blueprint for Success

Marriage, as instituted by God, comes with specific responsibilities for both husbands and wives. By fulfilling these roles, couples create a harmonious relationship that aligns with God's plan. Understanding these responsibilities is key to making a Christian marriage a success.

Responsibilities of Husbands

Spiritual Leadership

Key Scriptures: *Ephesians 5:22-23, 1 Corinthians 11:3*

The husband is identified as the head of the wife just as Christ is the head of the church (*Ephesians 5:23*). This doesn't mean domineering control but rather spiritual leadership. As head, the husband is responsible for the spiritual well-being of his family.

Practical Application:

Initiate family prayers, Bible study, and spiritual discussions. Lead by example in moral and ethical behavior.

84

HUSBANDS LOVE YOUR WIVES

Loving Their Wives

Key Scriptures: *Ephesians 5:25-28, Colossians 3:19*

Husbands are instructed to love their wives as Christ loved the church and gave Himself up for her (*Ephesians 5:25*). This entails a selfless, sacrificial love that seeks the best for the spouse.

Practical Application:

Be willing to make personal sacrifices for the good of your wife and family. Show compassion, understanding, and kindness.

Providing and Protecting

Key Scriptures: *1 Timothy 5:8, Ephesians 5:29*

It's a God-given responsibility for the husband to provide for his household (*1 Timothy 5:8*). This provision is not just material but also emotional and spiritual.

Practical Application:

Ensure financial stability, emotional support, and a secure environment for your wife and family.

Responsibilities of Wives

Submission and Respect

Key Scriptures: *Ephesians 5:22-24, 1 Peter 3:1-2*

Wives are instructed to submit to their husbands as unto the Lord (*Ephesians 5:22*). This submission is a sign of respect and it harmonizes the marital relationship.

Practical Application:

Acknowledge your husband's role as the family head and offer your support and counsel in decision-making.

Edward D. Andrews

Love and Emotional Support

Key Scriptures: *Titus 2:3-5*, *Proverbs 31:10-12*

Though the Bible emphasizes the husband's role to love, it equally expects wives to love their husbands (*Titus 2:4*). A wife's love often manifests as emotional support.

Practical Application:

Be there to encourage and uplift your husband, especially in times of stress or difficulty.

Home Management

Key Scriptures: *Proverbs 31:27*, *1 Timothy 5:14*

The Scriptures outline a role for the wife in managing the home. A wife should watch over household affairs diligently (*Proverbs 31:27*).

Practical Application:

Manage the household efficiently to create a peaceful and loving environment.

Mutual Responsibilities

Faithfulness and Integrity

Key Scriptures: *Hebrews 13:4*, *Proverbs 5:15-20*

Both partners are instructed to be faithful in marriage (*Hebrews 13:4*). Maintaining the marriage vows with integrity is a joint responsibility.

Practical Application:

Maintain loyalty to your spouse both in action and in thought.

Prayer and Spiritual Growth

Key Scriptures: *Matthew 18:19-20, 1 Thessalonians 5:17*

The couple should be united in prayer and spiritual pursuits (*Matthew 18:19*). This fosters unity and spiritual growth.

Practical Application:

Pray together for each other, for your family, and for wisdom in leading a Christian life.

Upholding God's Design for Marriage

God's blueprint for marriage provides roles and responsibilities that, when followed, create a relationship that honors Him. By each spouse fulfilling their God-given roles, they not only glorify God but also lay the foundation for a successful Christian marriage.

The Imperative of Love and Tenderness in Marriage

Love and tenderness are not just optional virtues in a marital relationship; they are biblical imperatives that God has outlined for the well-being and functionality of a marriage. The union between a husband and wife is often used in Scripture to typify the relationship between Christ and the Church, making the inclusion of love and tenderness even more vital.

The Biblical Foundation of Love in Marriage

Key Scriptures: *Ephesians 5:25, 28-33; Colossians 3:19; 1 Corinthians 13:1-8*

The Apostle Paul emphatically states in *Ephesians 5:25*, "Husbands, love your wives, as Christ loved the church and gave himself up for her." The love here is agape love, a

Edward D. Andrews

selfless, sacrificial, unconditional love. Similarly, wives are instructed in *Titus 2:4* to love their husbands. *1 Corinthians 13:1-8* gives a profound explanation of what love entails: it is patient, kind, and does not keep a record of wrongs, among other attributes.

Why Love is Important

1. **Fosters Unity**: Love promotes a sense of unity and partnership. It becomes the glue that holds the couple together in times of difficulty.

2. **Enhances Emotional Well-being**: Emotional needs are met when there is love in a marriage, leading to greater happiness and less stress.

3. **Builds Trust and Security**: Love inherently includes trust, a cornerstone in any marital relationship.

Practical Application

Demonstrate your love through actions, not just words. Acts of service, quality time, and physical touch are all expressions of love that contribute to a thriving marriage.

The Significance of Tenderness in Marriage

Key Scriptures: *1 Peter 3:7; Ephesians 4:32; Colossians 3:12-13*

Tenderness, or the quality of being gentle, kind, and affectionate, is essential for a fulfilling marital relationship. *1 Peter 3:7* mentions that husbands should live with their wives "in an understanding way, showing honor to the woman as the weaker vessel." *Ephesians 4:32* calls for believers to be "kind to one another, tenderhearted."

Why Tenderness is Important

1. **Smoothens Communication**: Tenderness makes communication easier and less likely to escalate into arguments or conflicts.

2. **Provides Emotional Safety**: It creates a secure emotional environment where both partners can be vulnerable without fear of ridicule or judgment.

3. **Nurtures and Sustains Love**: Tenderness is a way to express and sustain love over the long term, keeping the relationship from growing cold or distant.

Practical Application

Be considerate and gentle in your interactions with your spouse. This includes listening attentively and being responsive to each other's needs and concerns.

Love and Tenderness as Pillars of a Strong Marriage

It's clear that love and tenderness are more than just desirable traits; they are biblical mandates that God has instituted for the stability and happiness of marriage. By incorporating love and tenderness into the marital relationship, couples are not merely adhering to societal norms but are in fact obeying God's commands. These qualities ensure a strong, lasting, and spiritually fulfilling marital bond.

The Role of the Bible in Resolving Marital Problems

The Bible serves as an invaluable guide for resolving marital issues. The Word of God is "profitable for teaching, for reproof, for correction, and for training in righteousness" (2 Timothy 3:16). When marriage faces challenges, the Scripture provides timeless wisdom, principles, and practical advice that help in bringing resolution and peace.

Addressing the Root of Marital Problems

Key Scriptures: *Matthew 5:28; Ephesians 4:26-27; James 4:1-2*

Problems often stem from attitudes and behaviors contrary to the teachings of the Bible. For example, Jesus warns against looking at another person lustfully (Matthew 5:28), and Paul advises resolving anger before the day ends (Ephesians 4:26-27). James points out that fights and quarrels arise from sinful desires within (James 4:1-2).

Identification and Repentance

When marital issues surface, the Bible aids in identifying the root causes, whether it's pride, lust, or any other form of sin. True repentance involves turning away from sin and seeking God's forgiveness and guidance for change.

The Power of Prayer and God's Wisdom

Key Scriptures: *James 1:5; Philippians 4:6-7*

The Bible encourages seeking divine wisdom through prayer. James 1:5 states, "If any of you lacks wisdom, let him ask God." Additionally, *Philippians 4:6-7* emphasizes that we should present all our concerns to God in prayer, and His peace will guard our hearts and minds.

Divine Guidance

In times of marital strife, prayer should be the first line of defense. It enables the couple to seek divine intervention and guidance, and it places the problem in the hands of the One who can truly provide resolution.

Implementing Biblical Principles

Key Scriptures: *Ephesians 5:22-33; Colossians 3:18-19; 1 Peter 3:1-7*

The Bible is replete with principles on how husbands and wives should treat each other. Ephesians 5:22-33 gives detailed instructions, such as husbands loving their wives as Christ loved the Church and wives respecting their husbands.

Practical Application

By applying these principles in daily life, couples can preemptively prevent many issues that might otherwise arise. For those that do, these principles guide in resolving them in a manner pleasing to God.

The Bible as a Source of Comfort and Hope

Key Scriptures: *Romans 15:4; 2 Corinthians 1:3-4; Psalm 34:18*

Scripture also serves as a source of comfort and hope. It provides assurance that God is close to the brokenhearted and saves those who are crushed in spirit (Psalm 34:18). The comfort one receives from the Word can then be extended to their spouse, contributing to the healing process.

Emotional and Spiritual Support

During troubled times, the Bible uplifts the spirit and provides emotional stability. Its promises are anchors that can sustain a marriage through storms.

The Bible as the Ultimate Marital Guidebook

Edward D. Andrews

The Bible isn't just a book of doctrines; it's a practical guide for life, including marriage. When faced with problems, couples who turn to Scripture find not just guidelines but also the strength, wisdom, and comfort needed for resolution. Therefore, the Bible is an indispensable resource for any married couple facing challenges. It offers godly wisdom and provides the framework for a strong, godly marriage.

The First Priority of Christian Married Couples: Prioritizing God in Marriage

Christian marriage is a sacred covenant not just between two individuals, but also with God. Therefore, the first and foremost priority for Christian married couples should be to **honor God in their marriage**.

Obedience to God's Commandments

Key Scriptures: *Deuteronomy 6:5; Matthew 22:37-38*

The Greatest Commandment is to "love the Lord your God with all your heart and with all your soul and with all your mind" (Matthew 22:37-38). In the context of marriage, this means putting God first, above each other and above all else.

Living According to Biblical Principles

Obedience to God is not merely a matter of abstinence from sinful behaviors; it is also a proactive pursuit of righteousness. Couples should seek to apply biblical principles in all facets of their marriage, from communication to conflict resolution, and from intimacy to family planning.

Joint Spiritual Activities

Key Scriptures: *Matthew 18:20; Hebrews 10:24-25*

Christ promised that "where two or three are gathered in my name, there am I among them" (Matthew 18:20). Joint spiritual activities like prayer, Bible study, and corporate worship not only deepen the couple's relationship with God but also with each other.

The Role of Prayer and Bible Study

Prayer and Bible study should be fundamental practices in a Christian marriage. Couples should pray not just for each other, but with each other. Such activities enhance spiritual intimacy and are critical in keeping God as the central focus of the marriage.

Serving God Together

Key Scriptures: *Ephesians 2:10; 1 Peter 4:10*

Ephesians 2:10 tells us that "we are God's workmanship, created in Christ Jesus for good works." As a married couple, these good works extend beyond individual service into joint ministry opportunities.

Mutual Ministry

Married couples have unique opportunities to serve together, be it in the church, in missions, or in community service. This joint service not only honors God but also strengthens the marital bond.

Impact on Children

Key Scriptures: *Proverbs 22:6; Ephesians 6:4*

For couples blessed with children, the priority of God in marriage extends to the family. Children raised in a God-centered home are more likely to "not depart from it" as they grow older (Proverbs 22:6).

A Godly Legacy

Prioritizing God in marriage sets a powerful example for children, imparting to them the importance of a personal relationship with Christ. This creates a cycle of godliness that can extend to future generations.

The Essence of a God-Centered Marriage

Making God the priority in marriage yields numerous benefits: it provides a stable foundation, enhances marital satisfaction, and offers eternal rewards. More importantly, a marriage centered on God glorifies Him, which is the ultimate purpose of our lives and therefore should be the first priority of Christian married couples.

The Foundations for a Happy and Successful Christian Marriage

The notion that Christians can have a happy and successful marriage is rooted in the principles and teachings of the Scriptures. Below are the fundamental aspects that make this possible.

God-Designed Institution

Key Scriptures: *Genesis 2:24; Matthew 19:4-6*

Marriage was designed by God as revealed in the Book of Genesis: "Therefore a man shall leave his father and his mother and hold fast to his wife, and they shall become one flesh" (Genesis 2:24). Jesus reiterated this divine ordinance in Matthew 19:4-6. When the institution of marriage is understood as God-designed and God-ordained, it takes on a sanctity and seriousness that can contribute to its success and happiness.

God's Perfect Plan

In the divine design, each spouse has roles that complement the other, creating a partnership that reflects the relationship between Christ and the Church (Ephesians 5:22-33). Understanding and accepting these roles can lead to a harmonious marriage.

The Primacy of Love

Key Scriptures: *1 Corinthians 13:4-7; Ephesians 5:25*

Love, as described in the Bible, is patient, kind, and devoid of envy or pride (1 Corinthians 13:4-7). It is not self-serving but seeks the best for others. In Ephesians, husbands are explicitly commanded to love their wives as Christ loved the Church (Ephesians 5:25).

The Sustaining Power of Agape Love

This form of love, known as *agape*, is selfless and sacrificial. It is this kind of love that can sustain a marriage through thick and thin, making the marriage resilient and deeply satisfying.

Commitment and Covenant

Key Scriptures: *Malachi 2:14-16; Mark 10:9*

Marriage in the Christian context is a covenant, not just a social contract (Malachi 2:14-16). As such, it is binding and sacred. This covenantal view of marriage contributes to its longevity and success.

Lifelong Commitment

Edward D. Andrews

Understanding marriage as a lifelong commitment helps couples work through challenges instead of seeking an easy way out. "What therefore God has joined together, let not man separate" (Mark 10:9).

Practical Wisdom from the Scriptures

Key Scriptures: *James 1:5; Proverbs 24:3-4*

The Bible offers a wealth of practical advice and wisdom that can guide couples in their day-to-day life. "By wisdom a house is built, and by understanding it is established" (Proverbs 24:3-4).

Biblical Conflict Resolution

The Bible teaches ways to resolve conflict healthily and constructively, emphasizing forgiveness and reconciliation (Matthew 18:15-17; Ephesians 4:26-32).

Inclusion of God in the Marriage

Key Scriptures: *Matthew 6:33; Proverbs 3:5-6*

By including God in the marriage, seeking His Kingdom first, and relying on His wisdom, couples can build a stable and lasting relationship (Matthew 6:33; Proverbs 3:5-6).

Spiritual Unity

Couples who pray together, study the Bible together, and serve together experience a level of intimacy and unity that is deeply fulfilling and glorifying to God.

The Christian Advantage

Christians have a unique advantage in achieving a happy and successful marriage because they have access to divinely inspired principles, God's wisdom, and the grace that comes from a relationship with Jesus Christ. By adhering to the teachings of the Scriptures and maintaining a close relationship with God, Christian couples have the resources they need to build a resilient, fulfilling, and enduring marriage.

Edward D. Andrews

CHAPTER 6 What Husbands Can Do

The Role of the Husband in Marriage: A Biblical View

When it comes to marriage, the Scriptures are clear that both husband and wife have responsibilities to maintain a healthy and happy relationship. However, it is the husband who bears the greater responsibility due to his God-ordained role as the head of the family. The insights below expand on what this responsibility entails and how a husband can fulfill it.

The Concept of Headship

Key Scriptures: *Ephesians 5:23; 1 Corinthians 11:3*

Ephesians 5:23 unequivocally states, "For the husband is the head of the wife even as Christ is the head of the church, his body, and is himself its Savior." This headship isn't a license for tyranny or authoritarianism but a call for servant leadership that reflects Christ's relationship with the Church.

Understanding the Weight of Headship

The husband's headship carries a considerable weight of responsibility. It requires spiritual maturity and a depth of understanding of the Scriptures. The Apostle Paul compares this headship to how Christ is the head of the Church, setting an exceedingly high standard.

Love as the Guiding Principle
98

Key Scriptures: *Ephesians 5:25-29*

According to Ephesians 5:25-29, husbands are commanded to love their wives "as Christ loved the church and gave himself up for her." This implies a self-sacrificing love that places the wife's needs above the husband's own. Love is not merely an emotion but an ongoing action demonstrated through respectful and compassionate behavior.

Love's Manifestations

In a practical sense, love means being patient, understanding, and kind. It means taking the time to communicate openly, being willing to compromise, and always aiming to uplift and support the spouse.

Providing Spiritual Leadership

Key Scriptures: *1 Timothy 3:4-5; Joshua 24:15*

One of the chief responsibilities of a husband is to provide spiritual leadership in the home. In 1 Timothy 3:4-5, the qualifications for an overseer include managing his household well, which by implication applies to every Christian husband. Moreover, Joshua's declaration, "As for me and my house, we will serve the Lord" (Joshua 24:15), sets an example of how the husband should lead the family spiritually.

Conducting Family Worship

This spiritual leadership could manifest in conducting regular family Bible studies, leading in prayer, and ensuring that the family is involved in spiritual activities.

Financial and Emotional Support

Key Scriptures: *1 Timothy 5:8; Colossians 3:19*

The Scriptures explicitly state that a man who doesn't provide for his family has "denied the faith and is worse than an unbeliever" (1 Timothy 5:8). Emotional support is equally crucial. Colossians 3:19 instructs husbands not to be harsh with their wives.

Balancing Material and Emotional Needs

While it is important to provide materially, a husband should not neglect the emotional and psychological well-being of his wife.

Problem-Solving and Conflict Resolution

Key Scriptures: *Matthew 18:15-17; Ephesians 4:26-27*

The husband's role as the head also involves stepping up during conflicts to initiate resolution in line with Biblical principles. Matthew 18:15-17 and Ephesians 4:26-27 offer guidelines for resolving disputes righteously.

Tact and Timing in Addressing Issues

Approaching conflicts should be done wisely, ensuring that issues are not ignored but also not escalated unnecessarily.

Bearing the Mantle with Grace

The husband's role is laden with responsibilities that require great wisdom, love, and spiritual depth. When a husband understands and embraces his God-ordained role, the marriage not only fulfills its divine purpose but also brings happiness and fulfillment to both parties involved. The husband, in accepting his role, isn't just fulfilling a duty; he is directly contributing to the success and sanctity of the marriage.

What Husbands Can Do: A Biblical Guide to Marital Responsibilities

Marriage is a sacred institution, and the role of a husband within this covenantal relationship is clearly outlined in Scripture. God's Word provides explicit guidelines that help husbands fulfill their duties towards their wives and families. The primary roles include loving the wife as Christ loves the Church, acting as the spiritual leader of the home, and providing for the family's physical needs.

Love Your Wife as Christ Loves the Church

Key Scriptures: *Ephesians 5:25-33; Colossians 3:19*

The Depth of Christ's Love as a Model

Ephesians 5:25-33 sets the tone for what this love means, "Husbands, love your wives, as Christ loved the church and gave himself up for her." This kind of love is not superficial or conditional; it is selfless and sacrificial. This level of love reflects the kind of commitment that Christ has for the Church.

Demonstrating Active Love

Loving your wife means being there for her emotionally, physically, and spiritually. It means making her needs a priority and being willing to make sacrifices for her well-being. This love is also characterized by gentleness, as admonished in Colossians 3:19, "Husbands, love your wives, and do not be harsh with them."

Be the Spiritual Leader of Your Home

Edward D. Andrews

Key Scriptures: *Ephesians 6:4; Deuteronomy 6:6-9; 1 Timothy 3:4-5*

Guiding the Family in Faith

The Bible places the responsibility of spiritual leadership squarely on the shoulders of the husband. Ephesians 6:4 states, "Fathers, do not provoke your children to anger, but bring them up in the discipline and instruction of the Lord."

Implementing Spiritual Practices

Being a spiritual leader means more than merely going to church; it means nurturing the spiritual life of your family. This could involve leading family prayers, initiating Bible study sessions, and making decisions based on Biblical principles. Deuteronomy 6:6-9 emphasizes the importance of teaching the children and talking about the Scriptures at home.

Provide for Your Family's Physical Needs

Key Scriptures: *1 Timothy 5:8; 2 Thessalonians 3:10-12; Proverbs 22:29*

The Mandate to Provide

In 1 Timothy 5:8, we read, "But if anyone does not provide for his relatives, and especially for members of his household, he has denied the faith and is worse than an unbeliever." Providing for the family is not just a cultural expectation but a Biblical mandate.

Work Ethic and Provision

Work is not a consequence of the Fall but a divine ordinance (Genesis 2:15). A husband must be diligent in his work to provide for his family. This aligns with what is taught in 2 Thessalonians 3:10-12 and Proverbs 22:29, which both advocate for diligence and skillfulness in work.

Balance in Provision

While provision is essential, it should not come at the cost of neglecting other responsibilities. A balance must be maintained, ensuring that while providing for material needs, the emotional and spiritual needs are not sidelined.

Integrating Love, Leadership, and Provision

Being a husband according to the Biblical model is not a role to be taken lightly. It involves a multi-faceted approach that ensures the spiritual, emotional, and physical well-being of the family. When a husband embodies these principles, he aligns his marriage and family life with God's perfect plan, and in so doing, contributes significantly to the happiness, stability, and sanctity of the marriage.

What Husbands Can Do: Cultivating Communication, Affection, and Forgiveness

Husbands have an enormous responsibility in the Bible to lead, love, and support their families. But these broad roles are made up of many smaller, but equally significant, responsibilities that contribute to the harmony and success of a Christian marriage. We will explore four vital attributes that husbands should possess and practice: being a good listener and communicator, being affectionate and romantic, forgiving their wives when they make mistakes, and owning up to their own mistakes.

Be a Good Listener and Communicator

Edward D. Andrews

Key Scriptures: *James 1:19; Proverbs 18:13; Ephesians 4:29*

Importance of Active Listening

James 1:19 instructs us to be "quick to hear, slow to speak, slow to anger." Being a good listener is not merely about hearing but actively engaging in what your spouse is saying. Proverbs 18:13 warns, "If one gives an answer before he hears, it is his folly and shame."

Elements of Effective Communication

Effective communication goes beyond mere listening. It involves clarifying misunderstandings, asking questions, and providing thoughtful responses. Ephesians 4:29 exhorts us, "Let no corrupting talk come out of your mouths, but only such as is good for building up, as fits the occasion, that it may give grace to those who hear."

Be Affectionate and Romantic

Key Scriptures: *Song of Solomon 1:2; 1 Corinthians 7:3; Ephesians 5:28*

The Mandate for Marital Affection

The Song of Solomon beautifully portrays the depth of marital affection and romance. While some might shy away from discussing this, Scripture embraces it as part of a balanced marital relationship. "Let him kiss me with the kisses of his mouth! For your love is better than wine" (Song of Solomon 1:2).

Ongoing Romantic Engagement

Maintaining affection and romantic engagement isn't just for the honeymoon phase but should be sustained throughout the marriage. Ephesians 5:28 reminds husbands,

"In the same way, husbands should love their wives as their own bodies."

Forgive Your Wife When She Makes Mistakes

Key Scriptures: *Matthew 6:14-15; Colossians 3:13*

The Principle of Forgiveness

Forgiveness is a divine mandate. Matthew 6:14-15 says, "For if you forgive others their trespasses, your heavenly Father will also forgive you, but if you do not forgive others their trespasses, neither will your Father forgive your trespasses."

Exercise Patience and Compassion

In the context of marriage, forgiving your wife when she makes mistakes is a demonstration of grace and compassion. Colossians 3:13 encourages us to "Bear with each other and forgive one another if any of you has a grievance against someone. Forgive as the Lord forgave you."

Own Your Own Mistakes

Key Scriptures: *Proverbs 28:13; 1 John 1:9; James 5:16*

The Necessity of Acknowledging Faults

The Bible is clear that confessing and owning our faults is crucial. Proverbs 28:13 states, "Whoever conceals his transgressions will not prosper, but he who confesses and forsakes them will obtain mercy."

The Healing Power of Confession

The act of confession isn't just an individualistic concept but holds tremendous value in strengthening relationships, including marriage. James 5:16 tells us to "confess your sins to one another and pray for one another, that you may be healed."

The Tapestry of a God-Honoring Marriage

When these four attributes are integrated into a husband's everyday life, they contribute immensely to a strong and vibrant marriage. They allow the husband to fulfill his God-given role effectively, honoring not just his wife but God as well. A husband's commitment to active listening and effective communication, sustaining affection and romance, extending forgiveness, and owning his mistakes can indeed make the marriage a reflection of Christ's relationship with the Church.

What Husbands Can Do: Key Aspects for Building a God-Honoring Marriage

The Scriptures provide an excellent framework for understanding the multifaceted role that a husband plays in a marriage. It's not just about authority but about nurturing, loving, supporting, and leading in a Christ-centered manner. We will explore five vital characteristics that husbands can cultivate: Leading with Love, Providing Emotional Support, Practicing Humility, Cherishing and Respecting their Wives, and Nurturing Spiritual Unity.

Lead with Love

Key Scriptures: *Ephesians 5:25-28; 1 Corinthians 13:4-7*

The Christ-Centered Model

Ephesians 5:25 commands, "Husbands, love your wives, as Christ loved the church and gave himself up for her." This sets a high standard, presenting Christ's self-sacrificial love for the church as the model that every Christian husband should emulate.

Love Is More Than a Feeling

According to 1 Corinthians 13:4-7, love is patient, kind, not envious, not boastful, and it keeps no record of wrongs. Thus, love is an action, not merely an emotion. It means serving your wife, making sacrifices for her well-being, and prioritizing her needs above your own.

Provide Emotional Support

Key Scriptures: *1 Peter 3:7; Romans 12:15*

Understanding and Compassion

In 1 Peter 3:7, husbands are urged to live with their wives "in an understanding way." This includes being emotionally present and supportive, especially in times of difficulty or emotional stress.

Rejoice and Mourn Together

Romans 12:15 instructs us to "Rejoice with those who rejoice; mourn with those who mourn." This principle can and should be applied within the marital relationship to show emotional support.

Practice Humility

Key Scriptures: *Philippians 2:3-4; James 4:6*

The Virtue of Humility

Philippians 2:3-4 teaches us to "do nothing out of selfish ambition or vain conceit. Rather, in humility value others above yourselves." This should be evident in how a husband treats his wife, valuing her opinions, desires, and well-being.

Grace for the Humble

107

James 4:6 reminds us that "God opposes the proud but gives grace to the humble." Humility in marriage often means admitting when you're wrong and asking for forgiveness.

Cherish and Respect

Key Scriptures: *Proverbs 31:28-29; Ephesians 5:33*

The Call to Cherish

The virtuous woman of Proverbs 31 is said to be cherished by her husband: "Her children rise up and call her blessed; her husband also, and he praises her: 'Many women have done excellently, but you surpass them all.'" Cherishing your wife is about celebrating her uniqueness and praising her virtues.

The Element of Respect

Ephesians 5:33 instructs each husband to "love his wife as himself," while the wife must respect her husband. This mutual respect is the cornerstone of a healthy marital relationship.

Nurture Spiritual Unity

Key Scriptures: *Deuteronomy 6:6-7; Ephesians 5:26-27; 1 Peter 3:7*

Shared Spiritual Goals

Deuteronomy 6:6-7 urges parents to teach the commandments to their children. In a Christian marriage, nurturing spiritual unity means collectively studying Scripture, praying, and fostering a God-centered home.

The Husband's Role in Spiritual Nurturing

Ephesians 5:26-27 indicates that Christ cleanses and sanctifies the church. Similarly, husbands can play a role in the spiritual nurturing of their wives by encouraging her in her walk with God and ensuring the family's spiritual well-being.

Conclusion: A Harmonious Symphony of Marital Responsibilities

Marriage is like a complex but beautiful symphony that requires various instruments playing in harmony. Each of these responsibilities—Leading with Love, Providing Emotional Support, Practicing Humility, Cherishing and Respecting, and Nurturing Spiritual Unity—is like a different instrument. When played in concert, under the guidance of the Master Composer, they produce the harmonious music of a God-honoring, Christ-centered marriage.

Edward D. Andrews

CHAPTER 7
Husbands—Recognize Christ's Headship

Measuring the Success of a Husband and Understanding the Divine Origin of Marriage

How Might the Success of a Husband Be Measured?

Scriptural Fidelity

Key Scriptures: *Ephesians 5:25-28; Colossians 3:19; 1 Peter 3:7*

Success for a Christian husband can primarily be measured by his fidelity to the scriptural mandates concerning his role in the marriage. Ephesians 5:25-28, for instance, sets the high bar of loving one's wife as Christ loved the Church. Therefore, a husband's willingness to sacrifice for his wife, to put her needs above his own, becomes a key metric of his success.

Spiritual Leadership

Key Scriptures: *Joshua 24:15; 1 Corinthians 11:3*

The husband's role as the spiritual leader of the home is another critical area for gauging success. Joshua's commitment in Joshua 24:15—"But as for me and my house, we will serve the Lord"—stands as an excellent model for every Christian husband.

Emotional and Physical Provision

110

Key Scriptures: *1 Timothy 5:8; Ephesians 5:28-29*

A husband's ability to provide for his family's physical and emotional needs is also an indicator of his success. The Apostle Paul states in 1 Timothy 5:8 that a man who does not provide for his family has denied the faith. Additionally, the husband's care for his wife's emotional and physical well-being, as urged in Ephesians 5:28-29, is a crucial measure of his success.

Communication and Conflict Resolution

Key Scriptures: *James 1:19; Ephesians 4:26-27*

Effective communication and conflict resolution are also key indicators. James 1:19 advises everyone to be "quick to hear, slow to speak, slow to anger." A husband's ability to apply these principles in marital communication is a sign of his successful leadership.

Why Is It Vital to Recognize that Marriage Is of Divine Origin?

Divine Blueprint

Key Scriptures: *Genesis 2:24; Matthew 19:4-6*

Understanding that marriage is of divine origin is fundamental to its success because it offers a blueprint for how the relationship should function. Genesis 2:24 establishes the initial model of marriage, where a man and woman become one flesh. This design is later reiterated by Jesus in Matthew 19:4-6, emphasizing the permanency and sacredness of the marital bond.

Spiritual Accountability

Key Scriptures: *Hebrews 13:4; Malachi 2:14-16*

Edward D. Andrews

The divine origin of marriage holds both husband and wife accountable to a higher standard—God's standard. Hebrews 13:4 states that the marriage bed should be kept undefiled, as God will judge the sexually immoral. Malachi 2:14-16 also speaks of the seriousness with which God views the covenant of marriage, warning against marital unfaithfulness.

A Model for Christ and the Church

Key Scriptures: *Ephesians 5:31-32*

Lastly, Paul mentions in Ephesians 5:31-32 that the mystery of marriage is profound, symbolizing the relationship between Christ and the Church. Recognizing the divine origin of marriage helps us to understand its ultimate purpose: to glorify God and to serve as a living model of the relationship between Christ and His Church.

Measuring a husband's success is not a superficial or worldly assessment, but one deeply rooted in Scriptural principles and commands. Similarly, recognizing the divine origin of marriage elevates the relationship to its rightful status, inviting the couple to conform to God's design and hold themselves accountable to His standards. Both these elements work synergistically to build a strong, lasting, and God-honoring marital relationship.

Jesus Christ as a Model for Husbands: Insights into Christlike Headship in Marriage

For Whom Does Jesus Serve Primarily as a Model?

Jesus as a Model for Husbands

Key Scriptures: *Ephesians 5:25-28; 1 Peter 2:21*

Jesus Christ serves primarily as a model for husbands in the context of marriage. Paul explicitly states this in Ephesians 5:25-28, where he commands husbands to love their wives "just as Christ also loved the church and gave Himself up for her." Furthermore, 1 Peter 2:21 tells us that Christ left us an example so that we should follow in His steps, which is universally applicable but has special significance for husbands in practicing Christlike headship.

What Makes Jesus Knowledgeable About Marriage?

Divine Origin and Ultimate Marriage

Key Scriptures: *Matthew 19:4-6; Revelation 19:7-9*

Jesus is knowledgeable about marriage because He was present at its institution in Genesis. He reaffirms the divine origin and intent of marriage in His earthly ministry (Matthew 19:4-6). Furthermore, He is part of the Godhead that designed marriage as a shadow of the ultimate union between Christ and His Church, as revealed in Revelation 19:7-9, where the marriage supper of the Lamb is described.

Who is Jesus' Figurative Wife, and How Should Husbands Treat Their Wives?

The Church as the Bride of Christ

Key Scriptures: *Revelation 21:9; Ephesians 5:25-27*

Jesus' figurative "wife" is the Church. Revelation 21:9 refers to the Church as the "Bride, the wife of the Lamb."

This imagery is foundational for understanding the responsibilities and roles within Christian marriage.

Christ's Example in Treatment

Key Scriptures: *Ephesians 5:25-28; Colossians 3:19*

According to Ephesians 5:25-28, husbands should treat their wives with sacrificial love, emulating Christ's love for His Church. This love is not based on feelings or conditions but is a deliberate act of the will. It's a love that seeks the highest good for the other. Colossians 3:19 further instructs husbands not to be harsh with their wives, emphasizing kindness and understanding.

Examples of Jesus' Treatment of His Disciples Illustrating Christlike Headship

Consideration and Compassion

Key Scriptures: *Mark 6:31-32; John 13:1-17*

When His disciples were tired and overworked, Jesus showed great consideration by saying, "Come away by yourselves to a desolate place and rest a while" (Mark 6:31-32). This instance indicates that a husband should be attentive to the needs of his wife, providing her with rest and rejuvenation when needed.

Servant Leadership

Key Scriptures: *John 13:1-17; Matthew 20:25-28*

Jesus washed His disciples' feet in John 13:1-17, setting an example of servant leadership. In a similar manner, husbands should not lord their authority over their wives but serve them with humility and love, consistent with Jesus' admonition in Matthew 20:25-28 about what true leadership looks like.

Emotional and Spiritual Support

Key Scriptures: *John 14:1; 16:33; Matthew 11:28-30*

Jesus often provided emotional and spiritual support to His disciples. For example, He comforted them by saying, "Let not your hearts be troubled" (John 14:1) and offered peace in times of trouble (John 16:33). Similarly, a husband should offer emotional and spiritual support to his wife, inviting her into a relationship characterized by mutual care and encouragement.

Jesus Christ serves as the ultimate model for husbands in how they should conduct themselves within the context of marriage. His knowledge of marriage stems from His divine nature and the fact that marriage itself points toward the ultimate union of Christ and His Church. His life provided numerous examples of loving, considerate leadership that today's husbands would do well to emulate. By following Christ's example, husbands not only enrich their marital relationships but also fulfill their God-given roles in a way that honors Him.

Biblical Guidelines for Husbands: Dwelling with Wives in an Honorable Manner

How Should Husbands Dwell with Their Wives?

The Principle of Understanding and Respect

Key Scriptures: *1 Peter 3:7; Ephesians 5:25-28; Colossians 3:19*

The apostle Peter provides specific counsel on this matter in 1 Peter 3:7, stating that husbands should "dwell with your wives according to knowledge, assigning them honor, as a weaker vessel, the feminine one." This encapsulates the idea of intellectual and emotional understanding, as well as the provision of due honor and respect. Ephesians 5:25-28 and Colossians 3:19 echo this sentiment, instructing husbands to love their wives unconditionally and not to be harsh with them.

What is Involved in Dwelling with Wives According to Knowledge?

Recognizing Individual Needs and Preferences

Key Scriptures: *1 Corinthians 7:3; Philippians 2:4*

Dwelling with one's wife according to knowledge involves understanding her unique needs, preferences, and even her weaknesses. The apostle Paul encourages marital intimacy in 1 Corinthians 7:3, which requires knowing your spouse well. Philippians 2:4 admonishes Christians to look not only to their own interests but also to the interests of others, a principle highly applicable in marriage.

Being Attuned to Emotional and Spiritual Needs

Key Scriptures: *Galatians 6:2; Ephesians 4:29-32*

It also involves being sensitive to her emotional and spiritual needs. Galatians 6:2 tells us to bear one another's burdens, and Ephesians 4:29-32 advises us to speak what is edifying and forgiving, aspects that apply well in the context of marriage.

Why Do Wives Deserve to Receive Honor?

Equal Value Before God

Key Scriptures: *Genesis 1:27; Galatians 3:28*

Wives deserve to receive honor because they are made in the image of God, just as their husbands are (Genesis 1:27). Furthermore, in the spiritual sense, "there is neither male nor female; for you are all one in Christ Jesus" (Galatians 3:28). Thus, wives hold equal value and dignity before God and are deserving of honor.

According to Peter, for What Reason Should Husbands Honor Their Wives?

Wives as the Weaker Vessel

Key Scriptures: *1 Peter 3:7*

Peter states that wives should be given honor as the "weaker vessel." This does not suggest any form of inferiority but highlights the husband's role in providing care, protection, and emotional support. The term "weaker vessel" refers more to the physical constitution and possibly some societal settings rather than an indication of inferior spiritual or intellectual capacity.

How Did Jesus Show Honor to Women?

Compassion, Respect, and Inclusivity

Key Scriptures: *John 8:1-11; Luke 10:38-42; John 4:1-26*

Jesus showed tremendous honor to women throughout His ministry. For example, He refused to condemn the adulterous woman brought before Him, instead challenging those without sin to cast the first stone (John 8:1-11). In His interaction with Martha and Mary,

Jesus honored Mary's choice to sit at His feet and learn, a privilege generally reserved for men (Luke 10:38-42). Additionally, His respectful conversation with the Samaritan woman at the well (John 4:1-26) challenged societal norms that discriminated against women and Samaritans.

Husbands are called to dwell with their wives according to an understanding and knowledge that involves a deep recognition of their needs, emotional, physical, and spiritual. Wives, being equal in the eyes of God, deserve to be honored and respected. Jesus, the ultimate example, showed us how to properly honor women by His actions of inclusivity, compassion, and respect. Following these guidelines not only makes for a harmonious marriage but also pleases God, who instituted this sacred union.

The Art of Counseling in Marriage: A Biblical Framework for Husbands

The Imperative for Counseling with Kind, Well-Chosen Words

Key Scriptures: *Ephesians 4:29; Proverbs 16:24; Colossians 4:6*

The Bible is replete with principles for effective communication, particularly within the context of marital relationships. Ephesians 4:29 says, "Let no corrupting talk come out of your mouths, but only such as is good for building up, as fits the occasion, that it may give grace to those who hear." This biblical mandate establishes the foundation for how husbands should counsel their wives — with kindness and well-chosen words that edify.

Why Kind Words?

The Softening Power of Kindness

Key Scriptures: *Proverbs 15:1; Proverbs 25:15*

The Bible extols the virtues of kind words. According to Proverbs 15:1, "A soft answer turns away wrath, but a harsh word stirs up anger." Kindness has the power to defuse tension and create an environment conducive to open discussion and mutual respect. Another Proverb, 25:15, states that "patience can persuade a prince, and soft speech can break bones." Kind words hold immense power.

Reflecting Christ's Love

Key Scriptures: *Ephesians 5:25-29; 1 Corinthians 16:14*

In Ephesians 5:25-29, Paul instructs husbands to "love your wives, as Christ loved the church and gave himself up for her." This sacrificial love should manifest itself in all interactions with one's wife, including counseling. Everything done in love, as stated in 1 Corinthians 16:14, becomes inherently gracious and constructive.

The Importance of Well-Chosen Words

Fostering Emotional and Spiritual Growth

Key Scriptures: *Colossians 3:16; James 3:2-5*

Words can either build up or break down. Colossians 3:16 encourages believers to "let the word of Christ dwell in you richly, teaching and admonishing one another in all wisdom." Wisdom, in this context, involves the judicious use of words that can lead to emotional and spiritual growth. James 3:2-5 further illustrates the power of the tongue and how it can steer the course of one's life, emphasizing the critical nature of well-chosen words.

Navigating Complex Issues with Sensitivity

Key Scriptures: *Proverbs 12:18; 16:21; James 1:19*

Life, and by extension, marriage, is complex. Problems are nuanced and emotions run deep. Proverbs 12:18 contrasts reckless words, which are like "sword thrusts," with the tongue of the wise, which "brings healing." Proverbs 16:21 adds, "The wise of heart is called discerning, and sweetness of speech increases persuasiveness." Moreover, James 1:19 urges us to be "quick to hear, slow to speak," implying that the art of choosing words wisely involves active listening.

The act of counseling one's wife with kind, well-chosen words is not merely a pragmatic strategy for marital harmony but a biblical imperative that reflects the very character of Christ. By being gentle in speech and wise in counsel, a husband can create a spiritually nourishing environment in which both he and his wife can flourish, ultimately glorifying God, who is the author of marriage.

CHAPTER 8 Godly Conduct Within the Family Circle

God's Arrangement for Ruling the Family Circle and the Shortcomings of Adam and Modern Man

God's Original Design for Family Leadership

Key Scriptures: *Ephesians 5:22-25; Genesis 2:18-24; 1 Corinthians 11:3*

God's arrangement for family governance is established clearly in Scripture. According to Ephesians 5:22-25, the husband is to be the head of the wife, as Christ is the head of the church. This is not an arbitrary dictum but a divine ordinance that traces back to the creation account. Genesis 2:18-24 tells us that woman was made from man and for man, not in a subjugating sense, but as a "helper" fit for him. As the Apostle Paul elaborates in 1 Corinthians 11:3, the head of every man is Christ, the head of a wife is her husband, and the head of Christ is God.

Adam's Failure in Exercising Proper Headship

Key Scriptures: *Genesis 3:1-19; Romans 5:12-19*

Adam, the first man, failed miserably in his role as the head of his family. When confronted by the serpent, Eve

121

Edward D. Andrews

was deceived and ate the forbidden fruit. Adam, instead of exerting spiritual leadership and dissuading Eve, abdicated his responsibility and ate the fruit as well (Genesis 3:1-6). This failure had profound theological and existential consequences. As Paul states in Romans 5:12-19, through Adam's disobedience, sin and death entered the world.

Neglect of Spiritual Leadership

Adam's most glaring shortcoming was his neglect of spiritual leadership. He was present during the conversation between Eve and the serpent but failed to intervene or provide spiritual guidance. This was a glaring failure in maintaining the divine arrangement for family leadership.

How Persons Today Fall Short

Abdication of Spiritual Responsibility

Key Scriptures: *1 Timothy 5:8; Ephesians 6:4; Titus 2:5*

Like Adam, many husbands and fathers today abdicate their God-given role as the spiritual leaders of their homes. They may be preoccupied with work, hobbies, or other pursuits, leaving the spiritual instruction of their families to the church or even to the wives. This is a direct contradiction to 1 Timothy 5:8, which posits that anyone who does not provide for his family has denied the faith and is worse than an unbeliever.

Passive Involvement in Family Affairs

Key Scriptures: *Proverbs 22:6; Deuteronomy 6:6-7*

Many men are involved passively, if at all, in the lives of their family members. This falls short of biblical prescriptions for active involvement in the instruction and discipline of children (Proverbs 22:6) and in the ongoing conversation about the things of God within the home (Deuteronomy 6:6-7).

Failure to Love and Honor the Wife

Key Scriptures: *Colossians 3:19; 1 Peter 3:7*

Finally, some husbands fall short in their treatment of their wives, failing to love them as Christ loved the church and gave Himself up for her (Ephesians 5:25). They might mistreat their wives or demean them, thereby violating Colossians 3:19, which instructs husbands to love their wives and not to be harsh with them.

In both the example of Adam and the shortcomings evident in modern man, the crux of the issue lies in the abdication or abuse of God-ordained family roles. The pattern set forth in Scripture is one of loving, sacrificial leadership on the part of the husband and father. Any deviation from this God-given order undermines the spiritual health of the family and, consequently, the broader community and church. It is vital to recognize these shortcomings and realign our family lives in accordance with God's Word.

Lofty Patterns for Marriage and Oneness

The institution of marriage and the concept of oneness within this sacred bond have specific, high standards outlined in the Scriptures. These are not mere human conventions but divine designs that should be revered and adhered to.

The Marriage Pattern in Creation

Edward D. Andrews

Key Scriptures: *Genesis 2:24; Matthew 19:4-6; Ephesians 5:31*

The original design of marriage, as depicted in the creation account in Genesis, sets a lofty pattern for marital oneness. Genesis 2:24 states, "Therefore a man shall leave his father and his mother and hold fast to his wife, and they shall become one flesh." This is reiterated by Jesus in Matthew 19:4-6 and quoted by Paul in Ephesians 5:31, emphasizing that this "one flesh" relationship is not just physical but also spiritual and emotional.

Permanence and Exclusivity

One vital element in this pattern is the permanence and exclusivity of the marriage bond. The words "hold fast to his wife" imply a steadfast loyalty and commitment to one's spouse.

The Christ-Church Model

Key Scriptures: *Ephesians 5:22-33; Revelation 19:7-9; Revelation 21:2, 9-11*

Paul elevates the understanding of marriage by likening it to the relationship between Christ and the Church (Ephesians 5:22-33). Just as Christ loved the church and gave himself up for her, husbands are to love their wives. Wives, on the other hand, are to respect and submit to their husbands as unto the Lord. This gives a sanctified and elevated view of marriage, raising it to the level of a divine covenant.

Self-Sacrificial Love

Christ's love for the Church models a self-sacrificial love that husbands ought to emulate. This love is not based on feelings or circumstances but is a deliberate choice, even to the point of sacrifice.

Oneness in Purpose and Spirit

Key Scriptures: *Amos 3:3; 1 Corinthians 1:10; Philippians 2:1-2; Ephesians 4:3*

The Bible frequently discusses the concept of oneness or unity, not just in the context of marriage but also in the broader context of relationships within the body of Christ. Amos 3:3 asks, "Do two walk together, unless they have agreed to meet?" This rhetorical question points to the necessity of oneness in purpose for any joint endeavor, including marriage. Paul's admonition in 1 Corinthians 1:10 for believers to be united in the same mind and the same judgment can be applied to the marital relationship as well. Ephesians 4:3 speaks about "maintaining the unity of the Spirit in the bond of peace," a principle equally valid in a marital context.

Emotional and Spiritual Unity

In a marital setting, oneness extends to emotional and spiritual unity. This kind of oneness is more than mere physical unity; it's a unity of purpose, direction, and even spiritual understanding.

The lofty patterns for marriage and oneness as outlined in Scripture are both challenging and inspiring. They call us to live up to divine standards, not merely human conventions or societal norms. The more closely we align our marriages with these biblical patterns, the more fulfilling and God-honoring our marital relationships will be.

Edward D. Andrews

The Necessity of a Family Head: Biblical and Practical Perspectives

The concept of headship within the family unit is deeply rooted in biblical teaching and is reflected in the practical functioning of various forms of human organization. The structure God has laid down for the family has a purpose that extends beyond mere tradition. This teaching is not about superiority or inequality but about the divine arrangement designed for harmony and effective governance.

The Biblical Imperative for Family Headship

Key Scriptures: *Ephesians 5:22-33; 1 Corinthians 11:3; 1 Peter 3:1-7; Colossians 3:18-21*

The Bible clearly teaches that the husband is the head of the wife as Christ is the head of the Church (Ephesians 5:23). This headship is not an arbitrary societal construct but a divine ordinance. Paul writes in 1 Corinthians 11:3, "But I want you to understand that the head of every man is Christ, the head of a wife is her husband, and the head of Christ is God."

Leadership as a Spiritual Duty

The responsibility of headship carries with it the obligation of spiritual leadership. Husbands are to lead their families in a manner that reflects Christ's relationship with the Church. They are called to love their wives sacrificially, to provide and to protect (Ephesians 5:25-30).

The Practical Necessity of a Singular Head

Practical Examples: *Two Presidents, Two Ship Captains, Two Chiefs in an Indian Tribe*

Just as a nation cannot have two presidents, a ship cannot have two captains, and an Indian tribe cannot have two chiefs, so a family benefits from having a singular head. The reason is simple: Decision-making is more efficient, and responsibility is clearly delineated.

Unity of Purpose and Direction

Having a single head in any organization ensures unity of purpose and direction. It avoids the pitfalls of divided leadership, where differing opinions can stall decision-making and create confusion.

How Men Differ from Women

Key Scriptures: *Genesis 2:18-25; 1 Peter 3:7*

It's important to clarify that difference does not mean inequality. Men and women are equal in value and dignity but have different roles and functions. For example, Peter refers to women as the "weaker vessel" (1 Peter 3:7), not in terms of value or capability, but often in terms of physical strength and emotional make-up.

Complementary Design

The Genesis account indicates that woman was made from man and for man—not as a subordinate but as a "helper fit for him" (Genesis 2:18). This complementary design facilitates the functioning of the family unit when everyone adheres to their God-given roles.

God's Design for Men to be Family Heads

Key Scriptures: *1 Timothy 3:4-5; Ephesians 6:4; Deuteronomy 6:6-9*

The Bible emphasizes that men should manage their households well (1 Timothy 3:4-5). Men are called to bring up their children "in the discipline and instruction of the Lord" (Ephesians 6:4). This implies not just authority but also the responsibility to provide spiritual guidance.

Leadership Qualities Inherent in Design

Men are often designed with qualities that are essential for leadership—such as decisiveness, strength, and a problem-solving orientation. While these traits can, of course, be found in women, they are particularly emphasized in the biblical description of masculine roles.

In both the biblical mandate and the practical necessity, having a family head serves to create order, unity, and effective governance within the household. This is not a matter of male superiority but of divine design, wherein the different yet complementary roles of men and women work together for the good of the family and the glory of God.

The Exacting Duties and Many Obligations of Husbands in Proper Headship

Being a husband is not merely a title; it's a calling filled with numerous responsibilities and duties. These are both practical and spiritual, drawing heavily from the scriptural mandate for husbands to act as heads of their households. The role is demanding, and there is a heavy weight of obligation, but it's a godly calling that can yield much fruit when undertaken with wisdom and humility.

Exacting Duties: Scriptural Examples

Loving Sacrificially

Key Scripture: *Ephesians 5:25-27*

Ephesians 5 calls for husbands to love their wives just as Christ loved the Church and gave Himself up for her. This implies a love that is sacrificial, unconditional, and always looking out for the best interests of the spouse.

Providing Spiritual Leadership

Key Scripture: *1 Corinthians 14:35; Deuteronomy 6:6-9*

Husbands have the duty of leading their families spiritually. This involves not only instructing but modeling a godly lifestyle and taking the initiative in things like prayer and Bible study.

Managing the Household

Key Scripture: *1 Timothy 3:4-5*

In his letter to Timothy, Paul mentions that a man must manage his household well to be considered for the office of an overseer. Though not all men will be overseers, the principle remains: part of the husband's role is competent household management.

Protecting and Providing

Key Scripture: *1 Timothy 5:8*

The husband is tasked with being the primary provider for the family, ensuring that basic needs are met. This goes beyond just financial provision to include emotional and spiritual safety.

Edward D. Andrews

Obligations Attached to Proper Headship

Accountability Before God

Key Scripture: *Hebrews 13:17; James 3:1*

Being the head of the family means that a husband is accountable before God for the well-being and spiritual health of his family. This is a weighty obligation that should prompt careful thought and action.

Exercising Compassion and Understanding

Key Scripture: *1 Peter 3:7*

Peter calls for husbands to live with their wives in an understanding way, showing honor to them. Understanding and compassion are not optional; they are required of men who wish to fulfill their God-given roles effectively.

Nurturing and Encouraging

Key Scripture: *Colossians 3:19*

Colossians admonishes husbands not to be harsh with their wives but to love them. This includes nurturing their emotional and spiritual well-being and encouraging them in their own walk with God.

Leading Without Domineering

Key Scripture: *Matthew 20:25-28; Ephesians 5:28-29*

Christ's style of leadership was one of servanthood. Husbands are obligated to lead in a manner that is considerate and respects the dignity and worth of their wives. Leadership in the home is not an avenue for tyranny but an opportunity for service.

The role of a husband is indeed filled with exacting duties and many obligations. But when these duties and obligations are carried out in alignment with God's Word, the results are rewarding both for the individual and the family. Proper headship, modeled after Christ's relationship with the Church, brings about a loving, godly household that stands as a testament to God's wisdom and grace.

The Enduring Relevance of Biblical Counsel for Family Roles

In a world where traditional family roles and responsibilities are often questioned or even ridiculed, it's crucial to evaluate whether the Bible's teachings on these matters are outdated or impractical. Many argue that Scripture is out of touch with contemporary realities. However, a close examination shows that the Bible's counsel is not only relevant but also indispensable for the health and harmony of family life.

The Immutable Nature of God's Wisdom

Key Scripture: *Proverbs 2:6; James 1:5*

The wisdom that comes from God is unchanging and eternal. Just as physical laws like gravity have always been true, so have spiritual laws. God, being the creator of the family unit, knows what is best for its optimum functioning. His wisdom is practical and stands the test of time.

Universal Human Nature and Needs

Key Scripture: *Genesis 2:18-25; Ephesians 5:28-33*

Human nature and basic human needs have not changed over millennia. Men and women still have the same emotional, physical, and spiritual needs that they had in biblical times. The Bible's counsel addresses these unchanging aspects of humanity, offering solutions that are universally applicable.

Proven Success and Resilience of Biblically-Based Families

Key Scripture: *Psalm 128:1-4; Proverbs 22:6*

Empirical evidence, as well as numerous testimonials, demonstrate the resilience and success of families that adhere to biblical principles. Such families often exhibit stronger bonds, better communication, and a more profound sense of purpose and happiness. This cannot be mere coincidence but is indicative of the efficacy of biblical counsel.

The Deterioration of Families That Neglect Biblical Counsel

Key Scripture: *2 Timothy 3:1-5; Proverbs 14:12*

We live in an era where the neglect of biblical counsel has led to numerous societal problems, including broken families, and increased rates of divorce and domestic violence. These trends serve as a warning, showing what happens when God's guidelines are ignored.

Psychological and Sociological Support

Key Scripture: *Philippians 4:8-9; Romans 12:2*

Modern psychology and sociology often confirm the practicality of biblical counsel. For example, the idea of husbands loving their wives and wives respecting their husbands, as outlined in Ephesians 5, aligns with what many marital experts advise. When the Bible's principles are applied, the family benefits, and its members thrive.

Moral and Ethical Foundation

Key Scripture: *Deuteronomy 6:6-7; Proverbs 1:8-9*

The Bible provides a robust moral and ethical framework that is crucial for character development in children. Families that practice these principles are generally more cohesive and better equipped to navigate life's challenges.

The modern contention that the Bible's counsel is impractical for the family is not supported when one scrutinizes both Scripture and the evidence from real-world applications. On the contrary, biblical principles offer a timeless and universal guide that addresses the fundamental needs and challenges that families face. Far from being impractical or outdated, the Bible's teachings on family roles are both deeply relevant and profoundly effective.

The Consequences of a Wife's Refusal to Be Submissive and the Husband's Self-Examination

Understanding the dynamics of a marital relationship from a biblical perspective requires us to scrutinize both the roles of husbands and wives. When a wife refuses to be submissive, the ramifications can be significant, not only for her but for the family unit as a whole. However, it's crucial for the husband to first examine himself before passing judgment on his spouse's behavior.

Consequences of a Wife's Refusal to Be Submissive

Key Scripture: *Ephesians 5:22-24; 1 Peter 3:1-6*

1. **Breakdown of Biblical Order**: The Bible clearly outlines the roles within a family, with the husband

as the head and the wife being submissive to her husband. When this order is disrupted, it can lead to confusion, strife, and dysfunction within the family.

2. **Spiritual Ramifications**: The wife's insubordination can be indicative of a spiritual problem, impacting not just the relationship but her spiritual well-being.

3. **Impact on Children**: Children raised in such an environment may develop skewed understandings of biblical roles within the family, which they may carry into their future relationships.

4. **Erosion of Marital Unity**: The very essence of marital oneness could be jeopardized, as God designed marriage to operate in a particular order for it to function optimally.

Why Husbands Should First Examine Themselves

Key Scripture: *Ephesians 5:25-29; Colossians 3:19*

1. **Abusing Headship**: The role of a husband isn't that of a dictator. It is a role of love, care, and spiritual leadership. Abuse of this role could naturally lead to resistance from the wife.

2. **Being Oppressive**: A husband must not misuse his scriptural role to enforce oppressive or restrictive conditions upon his wife. Oppression will lead to resentment and, inevitably, lack of submission.

3. **Making Unwise Decisions**: As the spiritual leader, the husband is charged with making wise

choices for his family. If his decisions are consistently poor, it erodes the trust required for his wife to be submissive.

4. **Unbiblical Demands**: If a husband asks his wife to do something contrary to Scriptural teachings, her refusal to be submissive in such cases would be warranted. In such cases, the problem lies not with the wife but with the husband's understanding and application of Scripture.

Conducting a Self-Examination

2 Corinthians 13:5; Psalm 139:23-24

Before attributing a wife's lack of submission to her shortcomings, a husband must engage in serious self-examination. He should ask himself whether he is loving his wife "as Christ loved the church" and whether he is providing spiritual leadership that aligns with Scriptural principles. Only after this critical self-evaluation should he consider discussing his wife's role and responsibilities.

When a wife refuses to be submissive, it can lead to significant disruptions within the family unit, impacting its spiritual, emotional, and practical aspects. However, a wise and godly husband will first examine himself critically to ensure that he is not the one who is deviating from his Scriptural obligations, thereby leading his wife astray. This balanced approach ensures that both partners are aligning themselves with God's design for marriage, resulting in a more harmonious and spiritually fulfilling relationship.

Biblical Counsel Governing the Parent-Child Relationship

Navigating the intricate dynamics of parent-child relationships is challenging, yet the Bible provides robust guidance for both parents and children to foster harmonious family lives.

The Biblical Mandate for Parents and Children

Key Scripture: *Ephesians 6:1-4; Colossians 3:20-21; Proverbs 22:6*

1. **Children's Obedience**: Ephesians 6:1 instructs children to obey their parents "in the Lord," implying that obedience is within the context of godliness.

2. **Parental Nurturing**: Ephesians 6:4 and Colossians 3:21 counsel parents, particularly fathers, not to provoke their children to anger but to "bring them up in the discipline and instruction of the Lord."

3. **Train Up a Child**: Proverbs 22:6 advises parents to train a child in the way he should go, ensuring a foundation for future godliness.

Youths' Perspective on Adults and Vice Versa

Key Scripture: *2 Timothy 3:1-5; Proverbs 20:11*

1. **Disregard for Authority**: Many youths today exhibit a disregard for adult authority, aligning with 2 Timothy 3's prediction of people being disobedient to parents in the last days.

2. **Adults Underestimating Children**: Conversely, adults often underestimate the capabilities and

wisdom that can come from children, ignoring the wisdom in Proverbs 20:11 that even a child is known by his actions.

Guides are Better Than Rules

Key Scripture: *Proverbs 3:5-6; Galatians 5:22-23*

1. **Principles over Regulations**: Instead of a rigid set of rules, imparting godly principles allows children to make wise decisions based on a strong moral foundation.

2. **The Importance of Love**: Among these principles, love stands paramount. If children understand the principle of love, it governs their actions far better than any rule.

Guidance from Colossians 3:13-21, 23, 24

Key Scripture: *Colossians 3:13-21, 23, 24*

1. **Forgiveness and Love**: Verses 13-14 stress the necessity of forgiving each other and above all, putting on love, which binds everything together in harmony.

2. **Parents and Children**: Verses 20-21 explicitly address the parent-child relationship. Children are advised to obey their parents in everything, as it pleases the Lord. Fathers are warned not to provoke their children, lest they become discouraged.

3. **Work as Unto the Lord**: Verses 23-24 expand this principle beyond family dynamics, encouraging believers to work heartily, as for the Lord and not for men, teaching a valuable life lesson that can be instilled in children.

Edward D. Andrews

The Bible offers timeless wisdom for the parent-child relationship. Children are called to obey, and parents are cautioned against causing their children to become disheartened. In an age where respect for authority is waning, adhering to biblical principles can provide the much-needed framework for a stable family life. Rather than relying solely on rules, guiding children through godly principles—especially the principle of love—offers them a strong moral foundation for life.

CHAPTER 9 Lasting Gain from Living by the Bible as a Family

The Impact of Parental Adherence or Neglect of Bible Counsel on Children

The choices parents make in applying or ignoring biblical counsel have far-reaching consequences on the lives of their children. We find ample Scriptural evidence to support the claim that the spiritual and moral environment in the home shapes the next generation.

The Fruit of Following Biblical Counsel

Key Scripture: *Deuteronomy 6:6-9; Proverbs 22:6; Ephesians 6:4*

1. **Spiritual Formation**: Deuteronomy 6:6-9 prescribes the importance of keeping the commandments of God and teaching them diligently to children. This sets the stage for the child's spiritual formation, helping them internalize godly values.

2. **Secure Foundations**: Proverbs 22:6 suggests that training a child in the way he should go ensures that he will not depart from it when he is older. This speaks to the long-term stability and ethical direction in a child's life.

Edward D. Andrews

3. **Healthy Relationships**: Ephesians 6:4 advises fathers not to provoke their children to wrath but to bring them up in the training and admonition of the Lord. This fosters healthy family dynamics and emotional well-being for the children.

The Repercussions of Ignoring Biblical Counsel

Key Scripture: *Proverbs 29:15; Ephesians 6:4; Exodus 20:12*

1. **Moral Decay**: Proverbs 29:15 warns that a child left to himself will bring shame to his mother. The lack of moral and spiritual guidance could lead to the child adopting undesirable traits and habits.

2. **Emotional Scars**: Ignoring Ephesians 6:4's counsel can lead to children being provoked to wrath, resulting in emotional instability or long-lasting psychological scars.

3. **Loss of Blessings**: The fifth commandment in Exodus 20:12 promises blessings for honoring parents. However, if parents are not worthy of that honor due to neglecting their biblical duties, children lose out on this blessing.

Interpersonal and Societal Impact

Neglecting biblical principles can also lead to children having problematic relationships later in life, including within their own future families, thus perpetuating a cycle of dysfunction.

The extent to which parents apply or ignore Bible counsel has a direct and lasting impact on their children. Application of biblical principles leads to emotional, moral, and spiritual well-being in children, equipping them for challenges in life and fulfilling God's purpose for their lives.

On the other hand, neglect of these principles could lead to moral decay, emotional issues, and a life devoid of God's richest blessings. Therefore, the stakes are high, and the onus is on parents to take their Scriptural responsibilities seriously.

The Challenges of Properly Training Children in Today's World

In a world where secular humanism, relativism, and an array of other worldviews contest the Judeo-Christian ethic, the task of raising children in the "discipline and instruction of the Lord" (Ephesians 6:4, UASV) is decidedly challenging. Below, we will delve into some of the specific challenges that parents face when striving to train their children according to biblical standards.

Societal Values at Odds with Christian Morality

Key Scripture: Romans 12:2

The apostle Paul warns us not to be "conformed to this world, but be transformed by the renewing of your mind" (Romans 12:2). The values promoted by society, whether it be materialism, sexual liberation, or moral relativism, often run counter to Scriptural principles. Thus, parents have to work doubly hard to ensure that their children are not swayed by worldly ideologies.

The Influence of Technology and Social Media

Key Scripture: Philippians 4:8

The technological landscape has changed the way children consume information and interact with the world. While the Bible encourages us to think on things that are true, noble, and pure (Philippians 4:8), the unfiltered content available on the internet often presents viewpoints that are in direct conflict with biblical values.

Peer Pressure and the Desire for Social Acceptance

Key Scripture: Exodus 23:2; 1 Corinthians 15:33

Children, especially in their formative teen years, face intense pressure to conform to social norms. The Scriptures caution against following the crowd in doing wrong (Exodus 23:2) and remind us that "bad company corrupts good morals" (1 Corinthians 15:33). Navigating social dynamics while maintaining Christian principles is a complex challenge for children.

Academic and Extracurricular Pressures

Key Scripture: Matthew 6:33

The demands of academic and extracurricular activities can make it difficult for families to prioritize spiritual matters. Jesus admonished us to "seek first the kingdom of God" (Matthew 6:33). With an increasingly competitive world, however, parents and children alike often find it difficult to focus on spiritual education.

Declining Influence of Traditional Community and Church Structures

Key Scripture: Hebrews 10:25

The decline of the traditional church community as a constant in children's lives contributes to the difficulty. The Bible stresses the importance of not neglecting to meet together as a community of believers (Hebrews 10:25), but the societal trend is moving towards individualism and away from communal religious activities.

Internal Family Dynamics

Key Scripture: Colossians 3:21

The relationships within the family also play a crucial role in the child's development. Parents are warned not to provoke their children, lest they become discouraged (Colossians 3:21). A dysfunctional family environment can hamper the proper training of children in biblical principles.

In light of these challenges, the task of raising children in accordance with biblical principles is monumental but indispensable. Parents need to be vigilant, proactive, and deeply rooted in the Scriptures to successfully guide their children through the maze of contrary worldviews and ethical dilemmas they will undoubtedly face. The spiritual stakes are high, but the rewards, both earthly and eternal, are invaluable.

The Danger of Isolationism in Christian Families

The Scriptures repeatedly underscore the value of community, fellowship, and the sharing of life's burdens and joys with one another. In that light, let's delve into why isolationism poses a significant threat to Christian individuals and families, particularly the children.

Privacy vs. Isolationism: The Crucial Difference

Key Scripture: Ecclesiastes 4:9-12

While privacy is the well-defined and respectable space one might require for personal growth, reflection, and individual responsibilities, isolationism is the deliberate and prolonged detachment from others—especially one's community of faith. Ecclesiastes 4:9-12 eloquently states,

"Two are better than one because they have a good reward for their labor. For if they fall, one will lift up his companion. But woe to him who is alone when he falls, for he has no one to help him up."

Measures Parents Can Take to Counteract Isolationism

Key Scripture: Proverbs 22:6

Parents have the crucial role of setting the family's emotional and social climate. They can encourage community involvement, maintain open channels of communication, and be role models for social behavior. As Proverbs 22:6 states, "Train up a child in the way he should go; even when he is old he will not depart from it." This training includes cultivating a balanced approach to social interactions and community engagements.

Practical Steps

1. **Frequent Family Devotions**: Use this time not only for Bible study but also for open discussion about life, fears, hopes, and challenges.

2. **Church and Community Involvement**: Encourage participation in church activities or community service.

3. **Supervised Technology Use**: Keep an eye on your children's online activities to ensure they are not fostering virtual worlds at the expense of real-life relationships.

How Children Isolate Themselves and the Subsequent Risks

Key Scripture: Proverbs 18:1

Children, particularly teenagers, may resort to isolationism for various reasons—peer pressure, social anxiety, or even rebellion against authority. Proverbs 18:1 warns, "Whoever isolates himself seeks his own desire; he breaks out against all sound judgment."

Detrimental Effects:

1. **Emotional and Spiritual Stagnation**: Isolation prevents children from experiencing the mutual edification that comes from being part of a community (Romans 14:19).

2. **Vulnerability to Sin and Temptation**: The lack of accountability can make isolated children more susceptible to sinful behavior (James 5:16).

3. **Mental Health Concerns**: Prolonged isolation can lead to depression, anxiety, and other mental health issues (Psalm 42:11).

Isolationism disrupts the divine plan for community and fellowship among believers. Parents must be vigilant and proactive to ensure that their children do not fall into the trap of isolationism, understanding that this not only has spiritual repercussions but also psychological and emotional ones. It is within the community, the body of Christ, that individuals find the fullest expression of what it means to be created in the image of God.

The Challenge of Understanding Children's Inner Worlds

Understanding the thoughts and feelings of children is one of the most challenging and crucial responsibilities of

Edward D. Andrews

Christian parenting. In this age of social disconnect and myriad distractions, even well-meaning parents can falter in this critical area. The failure to grasp a child's internal world can have long-lasting repercussions.

Lack of Open Communication

Key Scripture: James 1:19

The Bible encourages believers to be "quick to hear, slow to speak, slow to anger" (James 1:19). This principle is doubly essential in a parent-child relationship. Often, parents are quick to offer advice, issue commands, or impose discipline, forgetting that listening is a form of love and respect.

Misplaced Priorities and Over-Scheduling

Key Scripture: Ephesians 5:16

Time is of the essence, and the way parents manage it can either open or close channels of communication with their children. Ephesians 5:16 advises us to "make the best use of the time, because the days are evil." An overly busy schedule can crowd out those precious moments where real conversations can occur.

Dismissal of Child's Perspective

Key Scripture: 1 Peter 5:5

The Scripture teaches that "younger men be subject to the elders," but also adds that "all of you clothe yourselves with humility toward one another" (1 Peter 5:5). Often, parents can undermine a child's feelings or ideas by assuming they lack significance or value due to their age.

Failure to Create a Safe Emotional Environment

Key Scripture: Colossians 3:21

146

Colossians 3:21 warns, "Fathers, do not provoke your children, lest they become discouraged." If the home environment is fraught with tension, high expectations, or criticism, children may withhold their true thoughts and feelings for fear of reprimand or mockery.

Absence of Regular Check-Ins

Key Scripture: Deuteronomy 6:6-9

The Bible encourages us to discuss Scriptural principles when sitting at home, walking on the road, lying down, and getting up (Deuteronomy 6:6-9). By extension, regular dialogues about life's various aspects can allow children to open up gradually, revealing their inner world. The absence of these "spiritual touchpoints" can be a missed opportunity for deeper understanding.

Relying on Assumptions Rather Than Questions

Key Scripture: Proverbs 18:13

"He who gives an answer before he hears, it is folly and shame to him" (Proverbs 18:13). Parents sometimes think they know what's best for their children without actually inquiring about the child's own thoughts or feelings.

Understanding a child's inner world requires intentional effort, active listening, and the grace-filled application of Scriptural principles. A failure in this area can be detrimental to the child's emotional and spiritual development, as well as to the relational health of the family. Therefore, Christian parents must be ever vigilant and proactive in engaging with their children's inner worlds.

Edward D. Andrews

The Admonition to Fathers in Ephesians 6:4 and its Implications

The guidance given to fathers in Ephesians 6:4 is profound and, when properly understood and applied, can yield lasting benefits not only for children but also for the whole family structure. The verse reads: "Fathers, do not provoke your children to anger, but bring them up in the discipline and instruction of the Lord."

The Dual Command: Do Not Provoke and Bring Them Up

Key Scripture: Ephesians 6:4

The admonition in Ephesians 6:4 can be seen as a dual command: first, what not to do ("do not provoke your children to anger"), and second, what to do ("bring them up in the discipline and instruction of the Lord"). Both aspects deserve careful consideration.

The Consequences of Provoking Children to Anger

Key Scripture: Colossians 3:21

The Bible is clear that provoking children can lead to discouragement. Colossians 3:21 echoes a similar warning: "Fathers, do not provoke your children, lest they become discouraged." This discouragement can manifest in various forms such as rebellion, emotional withdrawal, and even long-lasting resentment towards the parent or the things of God.

Emotional and Spiritual Ramifications: A child who is provoked unnecessarily can develop emotional scars.

148

Such negative experiences can taint their view of God, equating His character with their earthly father's failings.

Erosion of Parent-Child Relationship: The trust and emotional bond between parent and child can be significantly eroded. A child provoked to anger may find it difficult to seek counsel from such a parent, thereby weakening the instructive role the parent is biblically mandated to have.

The Importance of Discipline and Instruction

Key Scripture: Proverbs 22:6

The positive part of the command — "bring them up in the discipline and instruction of the Lord" — aligns with Proverbs 22:6, which instructs: "Train up a child in the way he should go; even when he is old he will not depart from it."

Spiritual Formation: The concept of discipline here is not merely punitive but involves forming the child's character and values according to the principles laid out in Scripture.

The Role of Instruction: Beyond discipline, fathers are to actively instruct their children in the ways of the Lord. This instruction is not just factual but also moral and spiritual, aimed at helping children develop a deep, meaningful relationship with God.

Ephesians 6:4 is a vital Scripture that outlines the balanced approach Christian fathers must take in rearing their children. Ignoring this admonition can have severe emotional, relational, and spiritual consequences, impacting not just the child but also the wider family and church community. Therefore, understanding and applying this

Scripture should be of paramount concern to any Christian father seeking to fulfill his God-given role effectively.

The Effective Discipline of Children by Fathers: A Biblical Framework

Effective discipline is an essential part of a father's role in the family unit, and it's crucial that this discipline aligns with biblical principles to produce positive, long-lasting effects on children. This endeavor requires a blend of love, wisdom, and consistency. Let's explore what the Scriptures teach about effective fatherly discipline.

Discipline Rooted in Love

Key Scriptures: Proverb 3:12; Hebrews 12:6

Discipline is not just about punishment; it's an expression of love. Proverbs 3:12 states, "For the Lord reproves him whom he loves, as a father the son in whom he delights." Likewise, Hebrews 12:6 reminds us, "For the Lord disciplines the one he loves, and chastises every son whom he receives."

Core Principle: Discipline should never be confused with abuse or mistreatment. It should always emanate from a heart of love, aiming for the child's well-being.

Wisdom in Discipline

Key Scriptures: James 1:5; Ephesians 6:4

Wisdom is crucial in the art of discipline. Fathers are advised to seek wisdom from God, as James 1:5 recommends, "If any of you lacks wisdom, let him ask God, who gives generously to all without reproach, and it will be given him."

Discernment: Wisdom means assessing the situation carefully, distinguishing between childish mistakes and deliberate disobedience. Ephesians 6:4 warns against provoking children to anger, indicating the necessity for fathers to exercise discernment in discipline.

Consistency in Discipline

Key Scripture: Proverbs 13:24

Consistency is vital for effective discipline. Proverbs 13:24 says, "Whoever spares the rod hates his son, but he who loves him is diligent to discipline him."

Uniform Standards: Fathers must set clear and consistent boundaries. Inconsistent discipline can create confusion and insecurity, undermining the child's understanding of right and wrong.

Proactive Teaching

Key Scripture: Deuteronomy 6:6-9

Effective discipline involves more than reactive measures; it includes proactive teaching. Deuteronomy 6:6-9 emphasizes the importance of teaching God's commands diligently to one's children.

Cultivating Moral Values: Fathers must be proactive in imparting godly values and wisdom, ensuring that children have a moral compass to guide them.

The Role of Encouragement and Affirmation

Key Scripture: 1 Thessalonians 5:11

Fathers should balance discipline with encouragement and affirmation. As 1 Thessalonians 5:11 urges, "Therefore encourage one another and build one another up, just as you are doing."

Positive Reinforcement: This is not about shielding children from consequences but offering love and affirmation that fosters a positive self-view and receptivity to discipline.

Effective discipline is a multifaceted endeavor that requires love, wisdom, and consistency, all underscored by a proactive approach to teaching and the balancing act of encouragement and affirmation. Fathers who apply these principles are better equipped to discipline their children in ways that will have a lasting positive impact, helping them mature into responsible, godly adults.

The Imperative of a Father's Time Investment in His Children

The Scriptures, as well as empirical evidence, affirm the crucial importance of a father's time investment in his children. This is not simply a sentimental notion but a divine design and psychological necessity that has lasting ramifications on a child's emotional, spiritual, and psychological well-being. Let's dive into the multiple facets of why this is so.

Building Emotional Security

Key Scriptures: Psalms 103:13; Colossians 3:21

A father's presence is invaluable in instilling a sense of emotional security. The Bible tells us in Psalms 103:13, "As a father has compassion on his children, so Jehovah has compassion on those who fear him." This compassionate interaction forms the foundation of emotional security in a child.

Core Principle: Colossians 3:21 warns fathers not to "exasperate your children, so that they won't become discouraged." Emotional security is vital for the mental health of the child and a father's active presence plays a critical role in that.

Spiritual Formation

Key Scriptures: Ephesians 6:4; Deuteronomy 6:6-9

A father's spiritual leadership is pivotal. Ephesians 6:4 instructs fathers to "bring them up in the training and instruction of the Lord." Deuteronomy 6:6-9 also emphasizes the father's role in continually teaching his children God's commands.

Consequence: The absence of spiritual leadership from the father often results in a spiritual vacuum, leading children to seek guidance from less reliable sources.

Teaching Life Skills and Moral Values

Key Scriptures: Proverbs 22:6; 2 Timothy 3:15

Time spent together is an educational venture. Proverbs 22:6 advises, "Train up a child in the way he should go; even when he is old he will not depart from it."

Lasting Impact: This is not merely about survival skills but also moral virtues, ethical standards, and a worldview grounded in Scriptural truth.

Building a Father-Child Relationship

Key Scripture: Malachi 4:6

The significance of a strong father-child relationship is indicated in the prophetic words of Malachi 4:6: "He will turn the hearts of the parents to their children, and the hearts of the children to their parents."

Relational Investment: A father who spends quality time with his children is making an investment in a relationship that will pay spiritual and emotional dividends for generations.

Preparing for Adulthood

Key Scriptures: 1 Timothy 5:8; Ephesians 4:13-15

1 Timothy 5:8 asserts, "But if anyone does not provide for his relatives, and especially for members of his household, he has denied the faith and is worse than an unbeliever." This provision isn't merely financial; it's also emotional and spiritual.

Life Preparation: Fathers prepare their children for the responsibilities and challenges of adulthood. Time spent in guided activities, open conversations, and mutual endeavors facilitate this process.

The importance of a father's time investment in his children cannot be overstated. It has biblical endorsement and psychological validation. Fathers are not merely providers but nurturers, educators, and spiritual leaders in the lives of their children. The time invested accomplishes more than any material provision ever could: it shapes character, forges emotional bonds, and prepares the next generation for life's challenges and responsibilities according to God's design.

The Necessity and Mechanics of a Father's Daily Instruction to His Children

The Bible places a high priority on the role of the father in imparting instruction to his children. This isn't merely a casual mention or an optional add-on but a core requirement for effective, godly fatherhood. Here's a deep dive into what this daily instruction involves.

Scriptural Mandate for Daily Instruction

Key Scripture: Deuteronomy 6:6-9

Deuteronomy 6:6-9 makes it abundantly clear that the father's role is to consistently and diligently instruct his children in the ways of Jehovah: "These words, which I am commanding you today, shall be on your heart. You shall teach them diligently to your sons and shall talk of them when you sit in your house and when you walk by the way and when you lie down and when you rise up."

Core Principle: Daily instruction is not an option but a command from Jehovah for the spiritual well-being of the family unit.

Elements of Daily Instruction

Instruction in Godly Wisdom

Key Scriptures: Proverbs 1:8-9; Proverbs 4:1-4

These Scriptures emphasize the role of the father in imparting wisdom and understanding. These are not mere academic exercises but life lessons drawn from the Scriptures.

Moral and Ethical Training

Key Scriptures: Ephesians 6:1-4; Colossians 3:20-21

Fathers are also entrusted with the moral and ethical upbringing of their children. This involves more than merely laying down rules; it also includes explaining the ethical reasoning behind those rules.

Teaching Practical Skills

Key Scripture: 1 Timothy 5:8

According to the apostle Paul, providing for one's family is of utmost importance. This provision includes teaching children practical skills for everyday life.

Emotional Support and Encouragement

Key Scripture: 1 Thessalonians 2:11-12

Paul describes a father as one who encourages, comforts, and implores his children to live worthy lives. Emotional education is also part of a father's daily instruction.

The How-to's of Daily Instruction

Active Involvement and Engagement

Fathers must be proactive. This means initiating discussions, asking questions, and involving children in Bible study and prayer. Instruction is not to be outsourced; it is a father's primary responsibility.

Contextual and Opportunistic Teaching

Utilizing opportunities that daily life presents to impart godly wisdom and practical knowledge is crucial. It could be during a car ride, mealtime, or even while doing chores.

Balance and Sensitivity

A father should not be excessively rigid or lenient but should adapt his teaching style to suit the needs and temperaments of his children.

Use of Parables and Analogies

Jesus, the Master Teacher, often used parables to make complex truths understandable. Fathers can follow this example to make their instruction more relatable and impactful.

Consequences of Failing to Instruct

Failure in this regard leads to a void that other influences will quickly fill. Whether it be the secular world, peer pressure, or other unsavory influences, the absence of a father's instruction often leads to the children seeking guidance in the wrong places.

A father's daily instruction to his children is not merely a traditional or sentimental practice but a biblical mandate that holds substantial weight in shaping the spiritual, moral, and emotional foundation of the child. Fathers who obey this command from Jehovah are not only fulfilling their God-given roles but are also investing in the eternal future of their children.

The Imperative of Training Children Regardless of the Parent's Recent Bible Appreciation

The Bible makes it abundantly clear that parents, regardless of how long they have been acquainted with its teachings, bear a God-given responsibility to train their children in the ways of righteousness. Below, we explore the nuances of this duty, specifically for parents who have only recently come to appreciate the value of the Scriptures.

The Scriptural Mandate for Parental Training

Key Scriptures: Proverbs 22:6, Ephesians 6:4

Proverbs 22:6 admonishes, "Train up a child in the way he should go, Even when he is old he will not depart from it." Ephesians 6:4 adds, "Fathers, do not provoke your children to anger, but bring them up in the discipline and instruction of the Lord."

Core Principle: The Scriptures do not offer exemptions based on the parent's length of time in the faith; the obligation to train one's children is immediate and unequivocal.

The Challenges of Recent Conversion or Renewed Faith

"Making Up for Lost Time"

Parents who have recently come to appreciate the Bible's value may feel like they are "making up for lost time." While the feeling is understandable, it should not lead to extreme measures that could alienate or overwhelm the child.

Fighting Against External Influences

Newly committed parents may also have to contend with external influences that have already shaped or are shaping their children's beliefs and attitudes. However, it's never too late to steer the ship in the right direction.

Strategies for Effective Training

Start with Humility and Honesty

Acknowledge your newfound faith or revitalized commitment to your children. This is in line with James 5:16, which advocates for confessing your faults to one another.

Be Consistent but Not Overbearing

Consistency in applying Scriptural principles is key, as per James 1:25. However, being overbearing can lead to the child becoming "exasperated," contrary to the counsel in Ephesians 6:4.

Use Age-Appropriate Methods

Deuteronomy 6:6-7 provides a framework for teaching children at all times and in various settings. Tailor your instruction to your child's developmental stage for maximum impact.

Involve the Child in Your Own Learning Journey

Parents can make their own Scriptural studies a family affair. This would involve open discussions, shared readings, and collaborative prayers, allowing for a mutual spiritual growth as a family unit.

Pray for Wisdom

James 1:5 encourages us to pray for wisdom, which is especially essential when you are navigating the complexities of parenting.

No Time Like the Present: Immediate Benefits and Eternal Significance

While you might feel regretful for not starting sooner, remember that Jehovah's mercies are new every morning (Lamentations 3:22-23). Each day presents a fresh opportunity to guide your children toward a life that honors God. This has both immediate benefits in fostering a harmonious family life and eternal significance in shaping their spiritual destinies.

Coming late to the faith should not deter parents from their God-ordained role of raising their children in the admonition of the Lord. The mandate is immediate and the stakes are high, yet the rewards—both temporal and eternal—are immeasurable. With Jehovah's guidance and a

Edward D. Andrews

diligent application of Scriptural principles, parents can fulfill this most sacred duty effectively, regardless of when they started their own spiritual journey.

The Requirements and Benefits of Living by the Bible

Living by the Bible is not simply an act of personal piety; it is a commitment to a lifestyle and a worldview that impacts every facet of a believer's existence. This involves both requirements and rewards. Let's delve into what the Scriptures reveal about what is required of a person who seeks to live by the Word of God, and how such a person stands to benefit.

Requirements for Living by the Bible

Unwavering Faith in God and His Word

Key Scripture: Hebrews 11:6

Hebrews 11:6 tells us that "without faith it is impossible to please him, for whoever would draw near to God must believe that he exists and that he rewards those who seek him."

Core Principle: Faith is the foundational requirement for anyone aiming to live by the Bible. This is not a blind faith but an informed confidence based on evidence and trust in God's character.

Consistent Obedience to God's Commands

Key Scripture: James 1:22 "Do not merely listen to the word, and so deceive yourselves. Do what it says."

Core Principle: Obedience to the commands of Scripture is not optional; it's a defining characteristic of a true follower of God.

A Lifestyle of Repentance and Holiness

Key Scripture: Acts 3:19 "Repent, then, and turn to God, so that your sins may be wiped out, that times of refreshing may come from the Lord."

Core Principle: Repentance is not a one-time event but an ongoing disposition. A life committed to holiness is in alignment with God's moral and ethical laws.

A Heart for Service and Love

Key Scripture: Mark 12:30-31 "Love the Lord your God with all your heart and with all your soul and with all your mind and with all your strength...Love your neighbor as yourself."

Core Principle: The pursuit of God involves the two-pronged love for God and for other people. This is the embodiment of all the Law and the Prophets.

A Commitment to Prayer and Scripture Study

Key Scripture: 2 Timothy 2:15 "Do your best to present yourself to God as one approved, a worker who has no need to be ashamed, rightly handling the word of truth."

Core Principle: A consistent engagement with the Scriptures through study, and a regular practice of prayer, are essential for living a life that aligns with Biblical principles.

How Is One Benefited By Living By The Bible?

Inner Peace and Joy

Key Scripture: Philippians 4:7 "The peace of God, which transcends all understanding, will guard your hearts and your minds in Christ Jesus."

Divine Guidance and Wisdom

Key Scripture: Proverbs 3:5-6 "Trust in the Lord with all your heart and lean not on your own understanding; in all your ways submit to him, and he will make your paths straight."

Material and Spiritual Provision

Key Scripture: Matthew 6:33 "But seek first his kingdom and his righteousness, and all these things will be given to you as well."

Eternal Life

Key Scripture: John 3:16 "For God so loved the world, that he gave his only Son, that whoever believes in him should not perish but have eternal life."

Living by the Bible is not an endeavor for the faint-hearted. It demands everything: your heart, soul, mind, and strength. Yet the benefits are incomparable and eternal. It offers a life of peace, wisdom, provision, and the incomparable gift of eternal life in the presence of God. Therefore, despite the challenges and sacrifices required, the rewards of living by the Bible far outweigh any cost.

CHAPTER 10 Protect Your Family From Destructive Influences

Family is one of the central institutions that God has designed for human flourishing, but it is under assault from various quarters. As shepherds of their households, parents need to be vigilant in identifying and neutralizing these threats. Let's look at the key destructive influences that can threaten a family and how parents can strike the right balance in protecting their families.

Destructive Influences on the Family

The Worldly Culture

Key Scripture: 1 John 2:15-17 "Do not love the world or the things in the world. If anyone loves the world, the love of the Father is not in him."

Core Principle: Worldliness can subtly or overtly affect a family's values, priorities, and actions. This includes materialism, sexual immorality, and relativistic ethics that contradict Scriptural teachings.

Peer Pressure

Key Scripture: Proverbs 13:20 "He who walks with the wise grows wise, but a companion of fools suffers harm."

Edward D. Andrews

Core Principle: Negative influence from peers can sway family members, especially children, away from Biblical principles and into destructive behaviors.

False Teachings and Philosophies

Key Scripture: Colossians 2:8 "See to it that no one takes you captive by philosophy and empty deceit, according to human tradition, according to the elemental spirits of the world, and not according to Christ."

Core Principle: Ideologies and teachings that are contrary to the truths of Scripture can undermine a family's spiritual foundation.

Personal Sin and Weaknesses

Key Scripture: James 1:14-15 "But each person is tempted when he is lured and enticed by his own desire. Then desire when it has conceived gives birth to sin, and sin when it is fully grown brings forth death."

Core Principle: Every family member has inherent sinful tendencies that can lead to destructive behaviors or habits, negatively impacting the family unit.

The Devil's Schemes

Key Scripture: 1 Peter 5:8 "Be sober-minded; be watchful. Your adversary the devil prowls around like a roaring lion, seeking someone to devour."

Core Principle: Satan actively seeks to destroy Godly families, using various tactics such as division, temptation, and deceit.

164

Striking the Right Balance in Family Protection

Discernment without Isolation

Key Scripture: Philippians 1:9-10 "And it is my prayer that your love may abound more and more, with knowledge and all discernment, so that you may approve what is excellent."

Core Principle: Parents should practice discernment in what influences they allow but should not completely isolate their family from the world. The goal is engagement without assimilation.

Truth with Love

Key Scripture: Ephesians 4:15 "Rather, speaking the truth in love, we are to grow up in every way into him who is the head, into Christ."

Core Principle: Parents must teach their children Scriptural truths while also exemplifying the love of Christ. Severity without love can alienate family members.

Guidance without Control

Key Scripture: Galatians 5:1 "For freedom Christ has set us free; stand firm therefore, and do not submit again to a yoke of slavery."

Core Principle: Parents should guide their children according to Biblical principles but should not be overly controlling. The ultimate goal is to raise independent adults who choose to follow God.

Faith with Works

Key Scripture: James 2:17 "So also faith by itself, if it does not have works, is dead."

Core Principle: It's not enough to merely believe in the protective power of God. Parents should actively work in line with their faith to guard their family against harmful influences.

Conclusion

Destructive influences that threaten the family are multifaceted and pervasive. However, parents equipped with the wisdom and guidance of Scripture are well-placed to fend off these threats. The goal is not to create a fortress that shuts out all external influences but to build a home grounded in Biblical principles, able to withstand the challenges it will inevitably face.

Protecting Children from Woke Ideological Education: A Biblical Perspective

In today's complex social climate, parents face unprecedented challenges in raising their children according to the timeless principles of Scripture. Among these challenges is the incursion of "woke" ideological education into the school system, pushing agendas like critical race theory, gender ideology, and various forms of liberalism. These teachings stand in stark contrast to a biblical worldview. Let's explore how Christian parents can navigate this tricky landscape to protect their children.

Know What Your Children Are Learning

Key Scripture: Proverbs 22:6 "Train up a child in the way he should go; even when he is old he will not depart from it."

Core Principle: Parents should be actively involved in what their children are being taught. They should not hesitate to scrutinize lesson plans, textbooks, and school communication.

Counter-Educate with Scriptural Principles

Key Scripture: Ephesians 6:4 "Fathers, do not provoke your children to anger, but bring them up in the discipline and instruction of the Lord."

Core Principle: Counteract any unbiblical teachings with a strong foundation of biblical principles at home. Make the Bible and its teachings a regular part of your family life.

Be Aware of Subtle Influences

Key Scripture: 2 Corinthians 11:14-15 "And no wonder, for even Satan disguises himself as an angel of light. So it is no surprise if his servants, also, disguise themselves as servants of righteousness."

Core Principle: The danger often lies not in overt teachings but in subtle insinuations and activities designed to manipulate children's perceptions of self and reality, like the case of Jenny mentioned in your scenario.

Engage with Teachers and School Officials

Key Scripture: Matthew 10:16 "Behold, I am sending you out as sheep in the midst of wolves, so be wise as serpents and innocent as doves."

Core Principle: Maintain an active relationship with the teachers and staff at your child's school. Politely but firmly express any concerns you have about the ideological content of the education they are providing.

Consider Alternative Education Options

Key Scripture: Romans 12:2 "Do not be conformed to this world, but be transformed by the renewal of your mind, that by testing you may discern what is the will of God, what is good and acceptable and perfect."

Core Principle: Depending on the severity of the ideological indoctrination, parents may need to consider alternative educational options such as homeschooling or Christian schools that align with biblical values.

Legal Recourse and Civil Disobedience

Key Scripture: Acts 5:29 "But Peter and the apostles answered, 'We must obey God rather than men.'"

Core Principle: As last resorts, legal action or even civil disobedience may be necessary to protect your children. In the given case of Jenny, the parents had every biblical and moral right to protect their child from a dangerous and life-altering ideology.

Emotional and Spiritual Support

Key Scripture: 1 Thessalonians 5:11 "Therefore encourage one another and build one another up, just as you are doing."

Core Principle: Even when you take all the right steps, your child may still be influenced by destructive ideologies. Provide a strong emotional and spiritual support system at home, grounded in the love and teachings of Christ.

The Bible offers wisdom for every situation, including the modern challenges posed by ideological education contrary to biblical principles. Parents need to be vigilant, proactive, and rooted in the Word of God to effectively shield their children from these harmful influences. In extreme cases, like that of Jenny, the consequences of inaction can be devastating, altering a child's life in unimaginable ways. Therefore, it is imperative that parents take this stewardship seriously, trusting in God for wisdom and guidance.

The Reckoning of Jennifer: A Journey from Jenny to Johnny and Back Again

The Genesis of Confusion

It was a bright September morning when five-year-old Jenny crossed the threshold of Mrs. Winterton's kindergarten class. Mrs. Winterton, a staunch advocate for progressive ideologies, noticed Jenny playing with toy trucks. This, in her mind, was the *opportunity*—to mold and guide, though some would say manipulate, a young soul into a narrative deeply disconnected from Jenny's Christian upbringing.

"Jenny," Mrs. Winterton leaned down and whispered, "have you ever felt like you're really a boy inside? Remember, this is our little secret."

Over the next six years, a concerted, cultish effort unfolded within the school to steer Jenny away from her God-given identity. Worksheets, discussions, and counseling sessions were strategically employed to imprint upon Jenny that she was born into the wrong body.

When Hormones Speak Louder Than Words

At the vulnerable age of 12, the school initiated hormone therapy for Jenny, now going by Johnny. This chemical intervention marked her body and psyche in irreversible ways. Her voice deepened; body hair sprouted where it had never been.

The school finally decided to inform Jenny's parents—staunch, God-fearing Christians—of the "transformation."

"Jenny is now Johnny, and he's been undergoing hormone therapy for a while now," announced the principal. "We're also preparing for gender-reassignment surgery in two years."

Faith Versus System

"Absolutely not," Jenny's mother broke down in tears, clutching a Bible to her chest. "You are trying to destroy God's creation!"

"This is child abuse!" the father roared. "Jenny is a girl, created in the image of God!"

But their pleas fell on deaf ears. Labeling them as abusers, the school took them to court and won. Jenny was taken from her home and, at 14, underwent the irreversible surgery that detached her not just from her biological reality but also from her spiritual heritage.

Awakening

A decade passed. At 24, Jenny—living as Johnny—stumbled upon a Bible that had lain forgotten in her apartment. The words of Genesis leapt off the pages: "So God created man in his own image, in the image of God he created him; male and female he created them" (Genesis 1:27).

Her eyes swelled with tears. The years of ideological programming began to crumble. She realized she had been living a fabricated life, a distortion of the beautiful reality God had intended for her.

The Cost of Truth

Jenny's life turned into a cascade of psychiatric consultations and de-transition procedures. Yet, she was shattered to discover the irreversible havoc the hormone therapies had wrought—she would never bear children.

In a reckoning moment, Jenny took legal action against the school for grooming her into a life that robbed her of her most fundamental identity. After a tumultuous battle, the court ruled in her favor, awarding her three million dollars.

But what is the worth of three million dollars when your very essence has been stolen, manipulated, and destroyed?

Redeeming the Broken Pieces

Today, Jennifer lives a life of advocacy, warning parents and schools of the irreversible damage that ideological indoctrination can cause. While money can never replace what was stolen from her, her story serves as a cautionary tale—one of a life nearly ruined by a narrative that contradicted the fundamental biblical truths she had once held dear.

The words of Scripture that once comforted her family now provided her solace and a sense of mission: "Train up a child in the way he should go; even when he is old he will not depart from it" (Proverbs 22:6).

Though Jennifer cannot regain her lost years or her ability to bear children, she's found a renewed sense of purpose: to protect innocent lives from being ensnared by ideologies that defy God's beautiful design for human sexuality and identity.

The Inextinguishable Light

Jennifer found solace in her faith, finding her identity not in a cultural narrative but in her Creator. Her story, both heartbreaking and redeeming, serves as a stark reminder that when human designs conflict with Divine plans, the soul will inevitably yearn for the truth—a truth that can only be found in the sacred words of Scripture and the eternal love of God.

And so, Jennifer stands, a broken vessel, yet one that reflects the light of undeniable, Scriptural truth—a light that no amount of darkness can extinguish.

Preventative Measures for Protecting Children from Ideological Indoctrination

Open Communication Channels

First and foremost, parents must establish open lines of communication with their children. This means not merely talking *at* them but talking *with* them. "Train up a child in the way he should go; even when he is old he will not depart from it" (Proverbs 22:6). This training is a two-way street. Children should feel comfortable coming to their parents with any questions or concerns.

Vigilant Oversight of Educational Content

Parents should be vigilant in understanding what their children are being taught at school. This means reviewing textbooks, talking to teachers, and even sitting in classes if possible. If a curriculum is found to include elements contrary to biblical teachings, parents have a responsibility to take action—whether that means meeting with teachers, talking to administrators, or moving their child to a different educational setting.

Foster a Strong Biblical Foundation

Children should have a robust understanding of biblical principles from an early age. Daily family devotions, Scripture memorization, and candid discussions about biblical viewpoints on contemporary issues can lay a strong foundation. The Bible says, "These commandments that I give you today are to be on your hearts. Impress them on your children. Talk about them when you sit at home and when you walk along the road, when you lie down and when you get up" (Deuteronomy 6:6-7).

Teach Critical Thinking Skills

Teach your children not only *what* to think but *how* to think. This involves equipping them to assess an argument critically, to discern logical inconsistencies, and to identify manipulative tactics. Children who can think critically are less likely to be swept away by persuasive but flawed arguments.

Social Media and Peer Monitoring

Parents must be aware of not only what their children are being taught but also who they are associating with. Social media platforms are a hotbed for all kinds of ideologies. Ensure that your children understand the perils and pitfalls of using such platforms and monitor their usage.

Parental Involvement in School Activities

Being actively involved in school events and committees allows parents to be part of shaping the school

Edward D. Andrews

environment. It also enables them to know what ideological issues may be infiltrating the school setting.

Legal Recourse and Rights

Know your rights as a parent. When you disagree with a teacher's or school's ideological stance that contradicts biblical truths, it's essential to understand the legal protections available to you. Engage with legal organizations committed to protecting religious freedom if you encounter challenges.

Strong Support Systems

Cultivate a strong support system composed of like-minded families, your church community, and possibly even legal experts who can offer advice. The saying, "It takes a village to raise a child," has a grain of truth. A strong, biblically-minded community can offer invaluable support in standing against ideological indoctrination.

Alternatives to Public Education

Consider alternative education options like homeschooling or Christian schools that align with your biblical beliefs. "Do not be yoked together with unbelievers. For what do righteousness and wickedness have in common? Or what fellowship can light have with darkness?" (2 Corinthians 6:14).

Conclusion

Being proactive, vigilant, and biblically grounded are the keys to safeguarding your children from destructive ideological influences. These measures are not guarantees, but they significantly reduce the risk of your children falling prey to harmful ideologies. Your home must become a sanctuary of biblical truth in a world increasingly hostile to such values. By fortifying this sanctuary, you're doing your

God-given duty to protect and nurture the souls entrusted to your care.

The Exposure to Distorted Information on Sexual Matters at School

Today's educational landscape is fraught with pitfalls for young minds, especially when it comes to sexual education. Some schools, under the guise of being "progressive" or "inclusive," introduce sex education curriculums that promote ideologies contrary to Biblical principles. These can range from normalizing premarital sex to encouraging exploratory sexual behavior from an early age. Such distortions are often presented as "facts," leaving children confused and vulnerable. The Apostle Paul warned against such distortions, stating, "Let no one deceive you with empty words" (Ephesians 5:6).

Countering Sexual Misinformation

The best way to counteract sexual misinformation is through *clear, honest, and Biblical communication*. Parents should be the primary educators when it comes to sexual matters. By instilling a Biblical view of sexuality from a young age, children will be better equipped to discern falsehoods. Proverbs 22:6 says, "Train up a child in the way he should go; even when he is old he will not depart from it." Knowing the truth helps children recognize lies. Moreover, parents should stay informed about the curriculum taught at their child's school and, if necessary, seek alternative educational options that align with a Biblical worldview.

Biblical Insights on Sexual Matters

Edward D. Andrews

The Bible has much to say about sexual matters, presenting them within the context of marital commitment and mutual love. 1 Corinthians 7:2-3 advises, "But because of the temptation to sexual immorality, each man should have his own wife and each woman her own husband. The husband should give to his wife her conjugal rights, and likewise the wife to her husband." Hebrews 13:4 further emphasizes the sanctity of marital relations: "Let marriage be held in honor among all, and let the marriage bed be undefiled." The Bible clearly delineates sexual boundaries, emphasizing purity, fidelity, and the sacredness of the marriage covenant.

No Correlation Between Godly Knowledge and Immorality

Contrary to the notion that talking about sex will lead to sexual activity, *Biblically-grounded sexual education can serve as a protective measure*. When children understand the God-ordained purpose and boundaries of sexual relations, they are less likely to engage in immoral behavior. The Apostle Paul encouraged believers to "abstain from sexual immorality" and to "know how to control your own body in holiness and honor" (1 Thessalonians 4:3-4). Information grounded in God's Word serves to guide rather than tempt.

Progressive Education on Intimate Matters

Children should be taught about sexual matters progressively, in a manner appropriate to their age and level of understanding. Just as you wouldn't teach advanced calculus to a first-grader, there are appropriate times and ways to introduce various aspects of sexuality. The key is to be attentive and open, answering questions and providing guidance as the child matures. This can be likened to how Jesus tailored His teachings to His audience's level of spiritual maturity, stating in John 16:12, "I still have many things to say to you, but you cannot bear them now."

To conclude, we live in a world increasingly indifferent or even hostile to Biblical principles, especially regarding sexuality. It's imperative for parents to be vigilant, proactive, and grounded in the Word of God to guide their children effectively through the maze of sexual misinformation.

Made in the USA
Las Vegas, NV
08 April 2024

88416827R00104